The Boundaries in Financial and Non-Financial Reporting

Although the need to expand the boundaries of financial reporting has been discussed since the mid-1990s, little consideration has been given to the evolution and discourses of integrated reporting and of non-financial aspects. Yet, by investigating how an organisation defines its reporting boundaries, it is possible to understand what is truly 'valued' (or not) in its business model and in its value creation.

This innovative book reviews the guidelines and frameworks from the major relevant international organisations including: the International Accounting Standards Board, the Global Reporting Initiative, the Sustainability Accounting Standards Board, the International Integrated Reporting Council, the Carbon Disclosure Standards Board and the World Intellectual Capital Initiative, and analyses their development and impact on the boundaries of financial and non-financial reporting.

Illustrated with case studies and interviews with representatives of these organisations and with companies' responsibles, this concise volume makes a significant contribution to the future of reporting theory and practice. It will be of great interest to advanced students, researchers, practitioners and policy makers.

Laura Girella works with the IIRC where her responsibilities include strengthening the business case for integrated reporting and supporting the Italian market on its journey towards adopting IR. She holds a PhD in Accounting and Business Economics with the University of Ferrara (Italy) (2013). She has published works in Journal of Intellectual Capital, Financial Reporting and Journal of Management and Governance, as well as chapters in international books.

Routledge Focus on Accounting and Auditing

Advances in the fields of accounting and auditing as areas of research and education, alongside shifts in the global economy, present a constantly shifting environment. This presents challenges for scholars and practitioners trying to keep up with the latest important insights in both theory and professional practice. *Routledge Focus on Accounting and Auditing* presents concise texts on key topics in the world of accounting research.

Individually, each title in the series provides coverage of a key topic in accounting and auditing, whilst collectively the series forms a comprehensive collection across the discipline of accounting.

The Boundaries in Financial and Non-Financial Reporting
A Comparative Analysis of their Constitutive Role
Laura Girella

For more information about this series, please visit: www.routledge.com/Routledge-Focus-on-Accounting-and-Auditing/book-series/RFAA

The Boundaries in Financial and Non-Financial Reporting
A Comparative Analysis of their Constitutive Role

Laura Girella

LONDON AND NEW YORK

First published 2018
by Routledge
2 Park Square, Milton Park, Abingdon, Oxon OX14 4RN

and by Routledge
711 Third Avenue, New York, NY 10017

Routledge is an imprint of the Taylor & Francis Group, an informa business

© 2018 Laura Girella

The right of Laura Girella to be identified as author of this work
has been asserted by her in accordance with sections 77 and 78 of
the Copyright, Designs and Patents Act 1988.

All rights reserved. No part of this book may be reprinted
or reproduced or utilised in any form or by any electronic,
mechanical, or other means, now known or hereafter invented,
including photocopying and recording, or in any information
storage or retrieval system, without permission in writing from the
publishers.

Trademark notice: Product or corporate names may be trademarks
or registered trademarks, and are used only for identification and
explanation without intent to infringe.

British Library Cataloguing-in-Publication Data
A catalogue record for this book is available from the British Library

Library of Congress Cataloging-in-Publication Data
A catalog record for this book has been requested

ISBN: 978-1-138-58690-1 (hbk)
ISBN: 978-0-429-50434-1 (ebk)

Typeset Times New Roman
by Apex CoVantage, LLC

To my children Alessandro and Giorgia Aurora
and to my family

Contents

List of illustrations x
Foreword by Prof. Stefano Zambon xi
Acknowledgements xiii

1 Introduction 1

   1.1 Why a book on reporting boundaries? 1
   1.2 Method of research 3
   1.3 Organisation of the book 5
   1.4 Boundaries in social management studies: some preliminary remarks 6
   1.5 Transplanting concepts across disciplinary boundaries: a proposed interpretive framework 11

2 Boundaries in financial reporting 25

   2.1 Proprietary vs. entity theories 25
   2.2 The IASB and FASB views 27
   2.3 Some technical and measurement implications 34
         2.3.1 The case of special purpose entities 34
         2.3.2 Reporting boundaries and minority interests 37
   2.4 Conclusion 40

3 Boundaries in non-financial reporting 44

   3.1 The sustainability reporting approaches 45
         3.1.1 The GRI Guidelines, the GRI Boundary Protocol and the GRI Standards 45

viii Contents

    3.1.2 The CDSB discussion paper and Framework 51
    3.1.3 The GHG Protocol, the SASB Standards, the A4S Guidelines and the TFCD Recommendations 55
  3.2 The 'value creation'-based approaches 60
    3.2.1 The WICI Intangibles Framework 60
    3.2.2 The International Integrated Reporting <IR> Framework 64
  3.3 EU Directive no. 95/2014 on Non-Financial and Diversity Information 66
  3.4 Conclusion 67

4 From theory to practice: reporting boundaries from financial to integrated reporting and their professional implications   69

  4.1 From sustainability to integrated reports: maintenance or change of reporting boundaries? 69
  4.2 From annual to integrated reports (through intellectual capital): distance from and convergence to financial reporting boundaries? 73
  4.3 The hybrid approach 74
  4.4 A new dimension of the hybrid approach: the inclusion of the United Nations' Sustainable Development Goals 75
  4.5 Development of the reporting entity concept 76
    4.5.1 The function of the reporting entity concept 81
  4.6 The reporting boundary and the auditor 81
  4.7 Materiality and stakeholders 82
    4.7.1 The concept of materiality 82
    4.7.2 A babel of definitions 84
    4.7.3 Materiality judgements 85
    4.7.4 Implications of materiality for the reporting boundary 86
  4.8 Conclusion 87

5 The boundaries in financial and non-financial reporting: A colossus built on shaky foundations? 91

   5.1 Boundaries in financial and non-financial reporting: a comparison 91

   5.2 The boundaries of financial and non-financial reporting: concluding remarks 97

Name index   109
Subject index   112

Illustrations

Figures

1.1	Zambon's original scheme (1996)	15
1.2	Logical correlation between theory of the firm, accounting theory and income measurement in financial reporting	16
2.1	Interactions between IFRS 10, 11, 12 and IAS 28	31
5.1	The boundaries in financial reporting	100
5.2	The boundaries in non-financial reporting	101
5.3	Logical correlation between theories of the firm, accounting theories and income measurement in financial and non-financial reporting	103

Table

5.1	Comparison of the definitions of reporting boundaries in financial and non-financial reporting	92

Foreword

Apparently, the topic of "boundaries" applied to reporting is old-fashioned and remote from the current research interests of academia at an international level. However, on a closer look, this topic is directly or indirectly at the very heart of many debates regarding the shape and content of present-day practice and standardization of accounting, such as the scope of financial and non-financial accountability, the edges of the value creation process, the impact of the supply chain, and users' information needs.

Defining boundaries means outlining the margins of that special representation called "corporate reporting", identifying some of its fundamental measures and information, and revealing the level of response to external expectations as to disclosure. In short, boundaries characterise in an essential way, and indeed are "consubstantial" with, the "object" to be reported upon. In fact, setting the boundaries of reporting contributes to the determination of those in the organisation, to the clarification of "what is in and what is out", and thus has an effect on the real world in terms of evidencing responsibilities and the fulfilment of the diverse stakeholders' requests.

The topic of boundaries is therefore central to the construction of accounts and reports. On the other hand, it should not be forgotten that the latter are artifacts of the human mind, and hence they reflect the conceptualization of the object made over time by the professional, the regulator, or the theoretician.

In this sense, financial accounting is based on boundaries that over the course of time have shown a strong evolution, conditioning the numbers that compose statements, their classification and the very calculation of surplus and its nature. Examples of this evolution are, for instance, the disputes in consolidated accounts over the role and measurement of non-controlling (or minority) interests, the possible exclusion of subsidiaries with dissimilar activities or located abroad, the elimination of intercompany revenues, expenses and profits/losses, the calculation and disclosure of the so-called full goodwill; and, for individual company accounts, the proposals regarding the treatment of dividends distributed (Li, Staubus) or the cost of capital (Anthony) as explicit expenses.

Indeed, boundaries are even more relevant today. Whilst, until 20 years or so ago, accounts were only financial in nature, in more recent times the diversification of expectations on and around corporate organisations has favored the preparation of several innovative types of accounts and reporting. Intellectual capital and intangible capital statements; social, environmental and sustainability reports; and, more recently, integrated reports have become more widespread internationally and sometimes have even entered legislation (cf. European Directive no. 95/2014). This variety of accountability forms, which can be concisely referred to as "non-financial reporting", has exacerbated the necessity of understanding and possibly establishing boundaries that are consistent with the aims of the diverse reports and the responsibilities of organisations. Up to which points should direct and indirect gas emissions, impacts on territories and populations, influences on climate, effects on value chains and modifications of intangible capitals be reported?

This significant work by Laura Girella explores in a critical and comprehensive way the topic of boundaries in corporate reporting. Far from being "old stuff" (Zeff, 2005), the present examination of the role of boundaries in both financial and non-financial reporting provides an original and in-depth analysis, which contributes to a better appreciation and framing of an important issue that has implications for several "burning" questions of current reporting practice, standardization and, ultimately, conceptualization (e.g., reporting entity, notion of value, non-controlling interests, principles of materiality and comparability, conceptual framework). The comparative perspective adopted between the financial and non-financial realms is also insightful and thought-provoking, and it demonstrates that the path ahead to strengthening corporate reporting is still long.

After all, if setting boundaries is constitutive of reporting, then the aims and the usefulness of corporate financial and non-financial information is genetically affected by the boundaries of the reporting entity as perceived and identified by the actors involved in the process.

Prof. Stefano Zambon (PhD, LSE)
University of Ferrara, Italy

Bibliography

Zeff, S. A. (2005), The entity theory of recording goodwill in business combinations: Old stuff, *CPA Journal*, 75(10).

Acknowledgements

I would like to thank Prof. Stefano Zambon for his continuing mentoring, advice and motivation. I am indebted to Mr. Mario Abela for our fruitful and friendly discussions and his scholarly contribution to this work.

I am grateful to Mrs. Jacqueline Curthoys for her considerable editorial assistance. And finally, I am thankful to my partner and my kids for their lasting patience and emotional support.

1 Introduction

1.1 Why a book on reporting boundaries?

Boundaries represent nowadays probably one of the most debated topics internationally. The ways they are set determine in fact identities, who we are and who we are not, at the personal, emotional, cultural, economic, environmental and geographical levels. For example, one of the latest concepts that has been advanced (2009) is that of 'planetary boundaries'. It corresponds to nine Earth system processes that have boundaries and that thus, limit the spaces within which humanity can operate without creating irreparable risks in the environment. They mark the safe zones for humanity and for the planet. Drawing upon this notion, it appears clear that the processes that are put in place in order to cast (and to dissolve) boundaries bring along implications that are fundamental for the constitution, maintenance or destruction of identities.

The significance of boundaries in accounting is not different. In his seminal paper titled 'The margins of accounting', Miller stated that "by looking at the margins of accounting, we can understand how this influential body of expertise is formed and transformed" (Miller, 1998:618). Indeed, according to him, it is at the margins of the discipline where it interfaces with others, where innovations useful for addressing the challenges in existing practices can be found. Only a few years before, Abbott (1995) pointed out that a change in the mapping of professional jurisdictions "was the proper focus of studies of professions and happened most often at the edges of professional jurisdictions [. . .] they (the boundaries) were the zones of action because they were the zones of conflict" (Abbott, 1995:857). Lightfoot and Martinez (1995) called for research that reconceptualises "frontiers as zones of cross-cutting social networks [. . .] and recognizes both the important role that core-periphery interactions play in frontier studies, as well as the socially charged arena of intercultural or interethnic interactions in frontiers context" (Lightfoot and Martinez, 1995:474;487).

Applying these analogies of 'boundaries' and 'conflicts', a parallel observation can be made that an examination of the boundaries of reporting, of what is happening at those 'margins' and 'zones of conflict', can help elucidate and identify solutions to current reporting issues. The notion of 'map making' is a familiar metaphor in reporting where the accountant as the 'map maker' (Solomons, 1978) draws the lines of the territory of the reporting entity[1] and the 'other' that remains outside of those contours. Just as political boundaries are drawn and re-drawn on maps, the boundaries of reporting (and the reporting entity) continue to shift in the light of changing relationships between the organisation and other economic, environmental and social entities that lie outside it. Examining that zone where those boundaries dissolve and re-form provides a rich understanding of the dynamics of organisational objectives, the evolution of its business model, and how its performance and viability is constructed and communicated through the financial statements. That is, by investigating the rationales that lead organisations to define and to delineate the margins of reporting in a particular way, it is possible to understand what really 'counts' (and what does not) for the organisation in terms of its business model and 'value creation' narrative. By so doing, the organisation constructs its own 'theory of the firm' regardless of the logic, assumptions and rational of the neoclassical theory of the firm in economics (Coase, 1937).

Advancing from this position, the interpretative schemes set out by Zambon (1996) provide a means of analysing the relationship between economic reality, conceptualisation of the accounting object and financial accounting model, making it possible to understand the role and function of reporting boundaries. In addition, Zambon and Zan (2000) explore the linkages between theories of the firm, accounting theories and income measurement. Those approaches are synthesised later in this chapter and are combined with the concept of 'boundary transplantation'. Accordingly, this book offers an overview on how the boundaries of reporting have (or have not) changed in response to the broadening scope of reporting needs to address both financial and 'non-financial' information (sustainability, governance and intangibles) and the attempts to promote greater integration of information. Indeed, despite several claims advanced since the mid-1990s on the need to expand the boundaries of financial reporting (Lev and Zarowin, 1999), and some reflections on the impacts that these changes could have on the profession (Edwards et al., 1999), only marginal consideration has been given to the *means* by which such 'expansion' has been implemented vis-à-vis the evolution of non-financial discourses and practices. Only a number of peripheral works have addressed this issue by noting that the definition of boundaries in non-financial reporting mimics the approach in financial reporting. However, no interpretative frameworks have been put forward in order to understand the reasons for, and the ways through which, this mimesis occurs.

This book aims to begin the process of filling this void. It will provide an in-depth and comparative analysis of the conceptual frameworks, standards and guidelines that have been recently published by organisations and standard setters operating in the areas of financial and non-financial reporting in order to examine how the issue of 'reporting boundaries' has been *problematised* and addressed. These will be then confronted with the approaches that organisations adopt for boundaries' setting in annual, sustainability and integrated reports. Therefore, the book utilises boundaries or corporate reporting widely conceived as an analytical tool to explore and *problematise* the conceptual foundations of the current reporting model per se. In this respect, the present study aims to be original in that it differentiates itself from capital market research and critical accounting research as traditionally conceived, because it poses at the centre of the investigation not the economic or non-economic impact of financial numbers, but the conceptual consistency and soundness of one of the main features (i.e. the boundaries) of the financial and non-financial reporting apparatus. Accordingly, this work is evidence-based, where the source of such evidence is provided by the authoritative pronouncements, frameworks, standards and their practical implementation and not by large samples of statistical or social nature.

1.2 Method of research

Adopting an interpretivist approach, the book adopts a 'simple' textual analysis of significant documents. The relevant frameworks, standards and guidelines for financial and non-financial reporting issued by the main standard setters and framework developers as well as the cases of five organisations that have moved from annual to sustainability and integrated reports are reviewed and compared – with a specific focus on their requirements and guidance on the 'reporting boundary' or 'reporting scope'.

Although quite simple in nature, this approach is very much in line with that used by Annisette (2017) in order to understand how categories are constructed. In addition, this methodological choice is guided by an inductive approach where there are no 'pre-conditions' or 'pre-constituted view' (as it may be in the case of content analysis or similar methods particularly in a deductive approach), or to force an *a priori* relationship between financial and non-financial reporting (as can be the case where linguistic concepts are employed such as 'linguistic borrowing' (Haugen, 1950, or 'boundary rhetoric' (Journet, 1993 and others). To put it another way, similarly to most cases in comparative law, no controlled comparison has been undertaken. A so-called 'concept formation through multiple descriptions' methodological approach has been adopted, able to cast light on how analogous challenges are manifested and solutions are provided (Choudhry, 2007). This way, a focus is placed on potential similarities and differences among cases.

This is an important methodological point given that, as far as the author knows, this is the first time a comparative analysis on reporting boundaries has been conducted at a conceptual level, going beyond a mere analysis of language change or translation (Evans, 2004, 2010). Accordingly, it should proceed free from any *ex ante* interpretive bias. Furthermore, as a more general point, it is well established in the critical literature that it is discourse that 'fabriques' the object as it is dependent upon the actors' willingness to maintain or change a particular way of seeing it portrayed (Foucault, 1972). Or, to put it another way, it is in the 'immaterial voice that pronounces' or 'in the page that transcribes it' that dissimilar objects can coexist (Foucault, 1970).

For these reasons, the analysis carried out in this book is based on an in-depth reading of those sections of the documents that deal with the topic of 'reporting boundary' or 'reporting scope'. As part of that approach, the terms 'boundary' and 'scope' have been detected throughout the documents by means of word search engines. The underlying rationale for searching for both terms derives from the observation that they are sometimes used interchangeably. Once they have been located, the related sections have been analysed to understand how the definitions have been contextualised and constructed. The next step was to consider which are the constitutive elements, the conceptual significance and implications of the definitions, first in isolation and then in comparison. Finally, the observations derived from this investigation have been situated within the wider conceptual and interpretive scheme provided by this text. The same process has been followed for the examination of the reports as they shift from annual to sustainability and to integrated forms. Although it is recognised that this approach may limit the consideration of the sets of discourses embedded in the texts examined, it needs to be noted that the terms 'boundary' or 'scope' are defined in *ad hoc* manner and are typically not anchored to a broader conceptual framework.

The analysis of these documents was followed up with interviews. Seven semi-structured interviews involving a set of open questions were conducted over the period July 2017–January 2018 in writing, in person and via Skype. The questions were prepared and pre-sent to interviewees. The interviewees included key representatives of the framework and guideline developer organisations, as well as organisational representatives primarily responsible for the preparation of annual, sustainability and integrated reports. The choice of the interviewees focused on those members representing the reference points, both at the institutional and organisational levels, for the definition and identification of reporting boundaries. Details about interviewees are provided in Table 1. The topics covered during the conversations

Table 1

No.	Name*	Position	Interview date
1	Sean Gilbert	Leader of the Working Group of the GRI Boundary Protocol	January 2018
2	A	CEO and Lead Researcher, Centre for ESG Research, Denmark and one of the three authors of the CDSB Discussion Paper	January 2018
3	Kay Alwert	Kay Alwert, Owner and general manager, Alwert GmbH & Co. KG and 'core member' of the Arbeitkreis Wissensbilanz	January 2018
4	Prof. Stefano Zambon	Prof. Stefano Zambon, Global Chair, World Intellectual Capital Initiative (WICI)	January 2018
5	B	Former Technical Officer for Framework Development, IIRC	July 2017
6	C	Deputy Chief Sustainability Officer, Solvay	January 2018
7	D	Director of Sustainability, SAP	January 2018

*Some of the interviewees names have been replaced with codes to preserve anonymity.

with these representatives concerned the rationales that motivated them to address this topic in a particular way, the influence that these documents may have had on practice and their opinion of the main challenges that their organisations face in identifying and defining reporting boundaries according to the extant guidelines, standards and frameworks. As for the themes addressed in the interviews with organisational representatives, they refer to the processes that characterised the setting of boundaries, the eventual changes that have been made in the shift from annual to sustainability and integrated reports and the difficulties encountered in identifying and defining boundaries consistently according to the extant guidelines, standards and frameworks. The interviews lasted between 30 and 60 minutes each and were all recorded and transcribed (if conducted in person or via Skype). The transcriptions formed the basis of the analysis.

1.3 Organisation of the book

The book is structured as follows. The remainder of this Chapter presents an overview of the ways in which boundaries have been addressed in economics and in social management sciences. Then, the conceptual apparatus that will inform the book is summarised. Chapter 2 offers a review of the extant problems relating to the identification and definition of reporting boundaries in financial reporting. Moving from the initial conceptualisation of proprietary and entity theories, as applied to company and group reports, it illustrates which (if any) have been the progresses related to reporting boundaries delineation. The main pronouncements and standards issued by the International Accounting Standards Board (IASB) and the Financial Accounting Standards Board (FASB) are presented. It also proposes some insights on technical and measurement aspects, such as non-controlling (minority) interests and the consolidations procedures adopted.

Chapter 3 is devoted to the major developments in the reporting of non-financial information. More specifically, it addresses the proposals advanced in relation to the setting and definition of reporting boundaries by the main standard setters and framework developers operating in the field of sustainability: the Global Reporting Initiative (GRI), the Climate Disclosure Standards Board (CDSB), the Greenhouse Gas (GHG) Protocol, the Sustainability Accounting Standards Board (SASB), the Accounting for Sustainability (A4S) Project, and the Recommendations of the Task Force on Climate-related Disclosures (TFCD) of the Financial Stability Board; and in the field of value creation: the International Integrated Reporting Council (IIRC) and the World Intellectual Capital Initiative (WICI). EU Directive no. 95/2014 on Non-Financial and Diversity Information is also presented. The main similarities and differences between the proposals are outlined, and furthermore the chapter includes the real voices of some of the actors who illustrate the reasons that led them to adopt a certain approach over another.

Chapter 4 offers examples drawn from practice. By relying on interviews conducted with organisational representatives, as well as on case studies extracted from annual, sustainability and integrated reports, it illustrates how companies have evolved (or not) in the practice of boundary setting and its implications. Then, the critical role of materiality and of reporting entity is investigated.

Finally, Chapter 5 summarises and comparatively examines the principal similarities and differences that stem from the definition and identification of boundaries in financial and non-financial reporting. It also discusses the conclusions in terms of theoretical contribution and, most importantly, the prospects for scholars and professionals operating and researching in these arenas.

Overall, this work aims to contribute to the current literature and practice by offering a 'new' interpretative scheme for the examination of reporting boundaries. Such a scheme makes it possible to identify and explore what transformations (if any) are occurring 'at the margins', both of theories that are invoked to prescribe boundaries and of devices belonging to the financial and non-financial realms. It also raises more general implications for accounting and the theory of the firm.

1.4 Boundaries in social management studies: some preliminary remarks

The notion of boundary can be said to have gained momentum in social sciences over the last few decades, even though Marx (1963), Durkheim

(1965) and Weber (1978) were already referring to it to describe the dynamics of social life and to delineate the differences and tensions in human behaviour. More recently, in the fields of social sciences, it has been the subject of lively debate in anthropology and sociology. Contributions in these arenas have proliferated based on what Lightfoot and Martinez (1995) refer to as the "colonialist perspective of core-periphery developments" (Lightfoot and Martinez, 1995:471). This perceives boundaries (or frontiers) as being semi-permeable, delineating what stays inside from what lies outside, and thus filtering (and controlling) information exchange and goods movements. Cultural transformations and innovations move unilaterally from the centre to the periphery where people change their habits and adopt the traits of the dominant culture which is located at the centre. The literature on boundaries in sociology has developed along similar lines, revolving around the conceptualisation of categorisation and, in particular, on categorisation leading to inequality. Amongst the plethora of typologies that can and have been theorised according to this perspective (cultural, moral, sexual etc.), probably the most well-known has been that proposed by Lamont and Molnár (2002), namely symbolic and social boundaries. Symbolic boundaries refer to the "conceptual distinctions made by social actors to categorize objects, people, practices, and even time and space", while social boundaries represent the "objectified forms of social differences manifested in unequal access to and unequal distribution of resources (material and nonmaterial) and social opportunities" (Lamont and Molnár, 2002:168). According to the authors, it is the interplay between these two typologies of boundaries as well as the properties and mechanisms through which they come into existence, evolve and dissolve that embody the aspects to be investigated.

In the fields of economics and social management, different approaches have been encountered. In economics, the study of boundaries has usually been associated with the problem of where they should be set with reference to the firm. In other words, discussions have centred on the questions of where do the boundaries of the firm lie, and what are the implications of this. Indeed, as previously stated, the question of where to locate the boundaries is strictly intertwined with the fundamental questions of why do firms exist and what are their functions. In this respect, initial observations were proposed in the seminal work of Coase (1937), followed by Penrose (1959), Richardson (1972) and Williamson (1975), to mention only a few. Interestingly, for each of these authors the firm emerges as a result of different relationships established with and within the market, and by virtue of the diverse functions inherent to the notion of boundaries which can either separate or connect the firm with the actors that operate in the surrounding environment (i.e. customers, suppliers, competitors etc.). In order to answer the questions "Do firm boundaries affect the allocation of resources?" and

"What determines where firm boundaries are drawn?", Coase advanced the view that firms were created by the market and in particular as a result of frictions in the use of price mechanisms. Once established, they are demarcated and differentiated from the market by means of boundaries that rely on efficiency logics. Activities are internalised up to the point where the costs related to internal management equalise the costs of transacting in the market. Penrose (1959) conceived the firm as "a collection of productive resources the disposal of which between different uses and over time is determined by administrative decision" (p. 24) and, according to her, boundaries are therefore set depending on the nature of administrative responsibilities. The approach of Richardson (1972, 1998) distinguishes itself from the others since it does not relate to the firm–market dichotomy. Relying on the work of Penrose, he argued that capabilities underline activities, and their potential to fit with others, in turn, influences how the boundaries of the firm are set. A further specific aspect of Richardson's framework is the fundamental 'relational' aspect. Relationships that are created both within the firm (as local knowledge) but also with 'external actors', such as suppliers, customers and competitors, create a network through which competition is run. As opposed to Richardson, but similar to Coase, Williamson in his 1975 book conceives market and firms (that he refers to as 'hierarchies') as polar modes. This conceptualisation has been then somehow softened even though the firm, in his view, continues to be seen in terms of transactions and its boundaries are set where these transactions allow costs to be minimised.

More recently, Grossman and Hart (1986) have advanced the 'property rights' view. According to this view, the firm coincides with those assets under common ownership. Therefore, its boundaries depend on decisions of assets ownership.

Loasby (1998a, 1998b) expanded on the works by Penrose and Richardson. According to him, the close association between capabilities and know-how is central to productive activities. In addition, in the definition of capabilities he advanced a further distinction between direct and indirect 'know-how'. The relevance for boundary setting of relationships created between firms and the external environmental has been outlined, as well as the relevance of indirect capabilities (Araujo et al., 2003). As the authors maintain:

> Firms are multi-faceted entities and the definition of their boundaries depends largely on the aims and purposes of the observer. From this perspective, firms have a variety of boundaries depending on which aspect of the defining characteristics we wish to focus on.
>
> (Araujo et al., 2003:1270)

With the advent of the so-called 'knowledge economy', this strand of literature has developed into more 'resource-based' approaches (Prahalad and Hamel, 1990). These address the problem of where to locate the boundaries of a firm when horizontal diversification and vertical integration, and thus 'intangible assets' such as competencies and capabilities, are at stake (Afuah, 2001; Leiblein and Miller, 2003; Jacobides and Billinger, 2006). Indeed, if we move away from pure physical production and competition, the problem of boundaries becomes more compelling with implications that affect the internal architecture and functioning of firms as well as the external structure of markets. In this respect, concepts such as organisational competences and dynamic capabilities that rely on the ability of the firm to address the changes that occur in the environment have emerged (Nelson and Winter, 1982; Teece and Pisano, 1994; Teece et al., 1997; Dosi and Teece, 1998).

However, it is worth noting that boundaries and their expansion have not only been investigated in terms of increases (in size, products, markets or regions), but also singular approaches have been proposed for the examination of boundary extensions in terms of "paying attention to smaller and smaller detail and developing a finer grained pattern", or what is called 'fractal organisation' (Zimmerman and Hurst, 1993:339).

As the following section explores, the investigation of boundaries has not represented a focal point of attention in accounting. Some exceptions do exist. In the Italian tradition of Economia Aziendale, in the German one, and in the general European tradition of Business Economics, the conceptualisations of what constitute an 'azienda' (or business entity) and the several theories of the firm that derive from them have been crucial for the development of this discipline (Zappa, 1957; Giannessi, 1969; Zambon and Zan, 2000; Biondi et al., 2008; Biondi and Zambon, 2013). With the expansion of the Anglo-Saxon thought that adopts a more 'operational' view, the so-called 'orientation postulate' (Viganò, 1966; Zeff, 1978), this focus has somewhat declined. However, despite the long-standing debate around the concept of boundaries in Europe, their identification and definition is an issue that is far from being resolved. The case of 'co-operatives' as illustrated by Zan (1990) is, for example, an argument still to be further developed. Additional discussion will be devoted to this topic later.

The public sector has probably embodied one of the latest fields to address the problem of boundaries, even though the problem has always been present (Musolf and Seidman, 1980; Kaboolian, 1998). As Kettl (2006) points out:

> Boundaries have long played a central role in American public administration. In part, this is because boundaries are central to the

administrative process, as they define what organizations are responsible for doing what and what powers and functions lie elsewhere.

(Kettl, 2006:10)

Concerns related to the assignment of responsibilities and in general of the (knowledge-based) production process can be said to have also inspired (if not refreshed) the discussion in management and organisational studies. Despite the fact that examination of boundaries is not completely new to the scholars of these disciplines,[2] it is not a domain warranting a great deal of attention. As acknowledged by Heracleous (2004), until very recently boundaries have been interpreted as unproblematic. To put it another way, their social dimension as well as the effects that they can generate on organisational life and behaviour have been neglected. It is only with the strengthening of competition and, especially, of technologically-based competition, that the problems associated with the production and management of knowledge and innovation inside, outside and across the organisation have created ideas such as 'the boundaryless organisation' (Hirschhorn and Gilmore, 1992), 'knowledge specialisation' (Brusoni et al., 2001) and 'boundary objects' (Star, 1988). As a consequence, studies have proliferated to uncover and propose new conceptions of (organisational) boundaries and their related features (Santos and Eisenhardt, 2005) and, in general, reveal the configurations able to capture how they should be managed (negotiated/maintained/dissolved) in the light of shifting locus of R&D expertise (Pisano, 1990), new product development (Carlile, 2002) and the role that (financial and management) accounting could eventually play in this respect (Llewellyn, 1994).

Beyond the different ways the theme of boundaries has been explored within the various social management fields, more generally it has also been scrutinised with reference to disciplines themselves. How and where the demarcation between science from non-science should be drawn (Popper, 1957) and/or re-drawn (Gulbenkian Commission on the Restructuring of the Social Sciences, 1996) and with what implications has been considerably debated in social sciences. "Defining a discipline defines what lies beyond it" (Wallerstein as cited by Massey, 1999:6) – it defines identity. This occurs through differentiation, exclusion and isolation, that is to say through the constitutive power of the outside (Massey, 1999). In this respect, probably the most well-known contributions have been from Bourdieu (1975) in defining the scientific field and, more recently, by Gieryn with reference to 'boundary work' (1983). Bourdieu recognised that the scientific field is a "locus of competitive struggle" (p. 19) where the issue at stake is the scientific authority, conceived as technical capacity and social power. Similarly, Gieryn maintains that the need for demarcation, for conferring an epistemic privilege on a discipline, is ideological in nature as it stems from the (vested) interests of the individuals, the scientists, who operate in it. The boundaries are not rigid but flexible and socially constructed. Following this line of reasoning, other scholars such as Fuller (1991) suggest that the attempts to scientifically demarcate science from non-science have failed and that knowledge has to be seen as exercising a wordly power through which it rhetorically focuses the attention on how it represents the world, and away from how it intervenes in it. In other words, the aim of a discipline is to continue to be perceived as central to society and to maintain access to political and material resources. Likewise, Massey (1999) asserts that the definition of disciplines should occur through the understanding of their particularity in virtue of the interrelations they establish (with the other disciplines). This way, she advances, there should not be division on the basis of subject matters, but disciplines should be conceived as 'angles of approaches' (p. 7). Wallerstein (1995) refers to 'overlap' instead of multi-disciplinarity because the latter presupposes the existence and relevance of boundaries that should be overcome. Multi-disciplinarity builds on boundaries.

1.5 Transplanting concepts across disciplinary boundaries: a proposed interpretive framework

Despite the relevance that the concept of reporting boundaries has witnessed in social management studies, it is a topic that has generated little interest in the accounting and, more generally in financial accounting, literature. This is surprising given the role and function of the reporting boundary for such things as the object of reporting, determining the basis of consolidation for the reporting entity; understanding the business model and value creation narrative; and the consequential implications for investors. There have been a litany of corporate scandals that have attempted to shift risks outside the reporting boundary, which ultimately led to a massive destruction of value and loss of investor confidence (e.g. Enron and more in general the (mis) use of SPEs in the US and other countries, Pirelli's foray into Telecom in Italy, the toxic loan portfolios of several European banks in the wake of the Global Financial Crisis and subsequent government bail-outs, just to mention a few). As noted previously, there has been little scholarly attention to this topic. In the financial accounting field, few exceptions have been represented by the works by Walker (1978), Lefebvre and Lin (1991), Bensadon (2005), Walton (2006), Saccon (2008) and Nobes (2014). Walker (1978) reviewed the process for the development of IAS 3 *Consolidated Financial Statements* by the then-IASC and maintained that the final standard was the result of efforts to accommodate alternative views and national differences related to consolidated accounts, rather than any robust conceptual notion.

Indeed, with reference to the scope of consolidation, he points out that the Exposure Draft (1974) emphasised the notion of (stable) 'control' and that the dissimilarity of business activities was not a basis to preclude consolidation, but this latter concept was abandoned in the final standard. IAS 3 required entities to be excluded from consolidation if their business activities were inconsistent with those of the parent entity or other subsidiaries. In addition, along with the concept of 'control', that of 'ownership' also made its appearance, such that entities that were owned, even if not controlled, have to be consolidated. Nobes (2014) has offered a re-examination of the manner in which the concept of 'scope of consolidation' has changed over a century. He points out that the scope had initially been conceptualised in the US through the lens of 'ownership' ('substantially owned' initially and subsequently changed to 'majority owned'). In Europe, negotiations between Germany (who advanced the notion of legal control) and the UK (who favoured an economic entity approach) during the developments of the EU Seventh Directive led to a confused concept of 'control': they made reference both to the 'right of control' and to the 'actual exercise of control'. Nobes (2014) in his final assessment concludes that the current version of IFRS does not address this aspect in a clear way and that the ultimate proposal of 'power' in IFRS 10 is used in an ambiguous and redundant manner.

In terms of international and national regulations, Lefebvre and Lin (1991) have critically and comparatively examined the requirements advanced on the scope of consolidation by the EU Seventh Directive, IAS 27 and the Belgian Royal Decree on Consolidation. In comparing the first two, they maintain that the differences between the two documents are substantial (the former much more detailed, while the latter more vague). More recently, Saccon (2008) has investigated the evolution of the concept and of the practices related to the perimeter of consolidation in the international and national domains. Her aim is to identify the similarities and differences between the various approaches used over the years and to examine the effective implementation of these standards in the Italian context during the first transition by listed companies to IAS/IFRS. On the basis of an empirical investigation of more than 100 Italian listed groups, she found that, in line with the requirements of the international accounting standards, there has been a widening of the group, in that there has been a major recognition of *de facto* control, and instances of subsidiaries being excluded have reduced. Focusing on a national setting, Bensadon (2005) has examined the evolution of the concept in France and illustrated the difficulties encountered in order to draw the boundaries of a group by a multinational organisation over a period of 20 years. He notes how the French rules have distanced themselves from the Anglo-Saxon ones, how the notion of control has become much more sophisticated (especially by virtue of the law of 1985) and how the diversity of businesses between the parent company and the subsidiaries is an element that has been progressively abandoned. The merger with the commune Pont-à-Mousson, located in the Meurthe-et-Moselle department in north-east France, has represented a radical change towards more transparent financial statements, and the significant changes in the scope of consolidation are explained through pro-forma statement.

More generally, Walton (2006) has recognised how the change of boundaries in financial reporting, especially towards the adoption of fair value for executory contracts which leads to the recognition of a transaction before its completion, derives from the different conception of reliability and the prominence that accounting standard setters are giving to representation faithfulness rather than measurement certainty.

Within non-financial reporting, and in particular in environmental reporting, Archel et al. (2008) have investigated boundary setting with reference to Triple Bottom Line Reporting. Through a content analysis of around 50 best practice reports, they maintain that the vague nature of boundary setting determines a similar unclear notion of the reporting entity at the expense of accountability. Indeed, they found that the voluntary nature of this form of reporting, accompanied by a lack of prescription of how to set organisational boundaries, leads organisations to (strategically) decide what to disclose. Moneva et al. (2006) interpret the efforts of GRI to develop a Boundary Protocol in a similar vein, that is to hide the 'unsustainability' of the organisation. Anderson (2010), Young (2010) and Nelson et al. (2011) have analysed the particular case of the National Greenhouse and Energy Reporting Act released by the Department of Climate Change in Australia in 2007 (NGER) and have maintained that the criteria of 'operational control' as determinant for considering a group liable for a facility's emission is not robust enough and too narrow. With reference to the broader sustainability realm, Lamberton (2005), in an attempt to define a sustainability framework able to capture the developments occurred within the field, links the boundaries of a sustainability accounting system to the need to "limit the scope to a manageable exercise" (Lamberton, 2005:20).

If the realm of intellectual capital (IC) and of intangibles is examined, it is possible to note that several perspectives have been proposed with reference to boundaries, even though none of them can be seen as proposing a complete theoretical framework for analysis. Roos (1998) has advanced the view that the boundaries of the firm represent "the potential IC can access and put in use" (p. 152). In investigating the case of the COSA, a business unit of Caterpillar, he points out that its boundaries are embodied by those IC elements (knowledge, relationships) that "can be accessed and leveraged to make more money" (p. 152). In a similar manner, Bontis and Fitzenz (2002) have acknowledged that the boundaries of the firm designate its relational capital. Indeed, according to them relational capital is the knowledge embedded in the relationships that lie outside the boundaries of the firm (p. 225). Also Mouritsen et al. (2001) identify the value of intangibles as stemming from interactions "at the boundaries". They state that

> the boundary mobilised in the bottom line or in share prices is still there. However, the way this value is made to count is through the mobilisation of an image of a firm that thrives on relationships far beyond, in time and space, the value in the financial account.
>
> (p. 404)

In a more critical vein, Gowthorpe (2009) has contended that the traditional financial reporting and management accounting models cannot encompass the components of IC. Rather, the idea of a multiplicity of organisational boundaries as advanced by Grandori (2000) is able to better satisfy the different characteristics of IC management, measurement and reporting.

At the intersection between financial and 'non-financial' reporting, Meyssonnier and Pourtier (2013) recognise that only considering 'financial reporting' boundaries fails to provide a comprehensive picture of the company's economic reality. Accordingly, they suggest that IFRS 10, which in their view has made a relevant conceptual contribution in this respect, should be complemented with the disclosure of the accounting information and the cash flows that derive from the organisation's 'zone of influence'. Andrei (2007), Andrei and Pesci (2009) and Pesci and Andrei (2011) investigated the relationship between the definition of boundaries in corporate social responsibility reporting and financial reporting. Through an analysis of Italian practices, they found that there are still differentiated procedures, even though it is possible to note an emerging trend towards a coincidence between the two.

Despite the efforts noted previously, in the author's view these papers can be said to rely on a myopic perspective. Indeed, none of them have advanced theoretical frameworks able to extensively comprehend the logic and the complexities inherent in the topic. Furthermore, they mainly refer to either financial reporting or non-financial reporting but not both. Similarly, the paper by Meyssonnier and Pourtier (2013), which can be seen at the intersect between the two fields, does not provide a detailed picture of the developments in non-financial reporting. Along similar lines, the work by Andrei and Pesci (2009) and Pesci and Andrei (2011) has focused mainly on proposals advanced by GRI, has been primarily empirical in nature and fails to situate within a theoretical frame. Finally, as pointed out previously, although some works discuss that the boundaries in non-financial reporting mimic those in financial reporting (Archel et al., 2008; Kaspersen, 2013), the rationales for this are not explored. Drawing upon this paucity of investigation, the present work proposes a conceptual apparatus based on a combination of two interpretive schemes referred to consolidated financial statements and a concept drawn from comparative law. The conceptual frameworks used are the ones suggested by Zambon (1996) (Figure 1.1), which considers the relationships between economic reality, conceptualisation of the accounting object and the financial reporting basis for consolidation; and by Zambon and Zan (2000), on the relationship between theories of the firm, accounting theories and income measurement (Figure 1.2). The concept adopted from comparative law is the one of 'boundary transplantation'. The choice to use these frameworks and this concept and to combine them is twofold. Firstly, it relies on the simplicity of the Zambon (1996) and Zambon and Zan (2000) schemes and the possibility to adapt them also to non-financial reporting. Secondly, it relates to the implicit reference in the

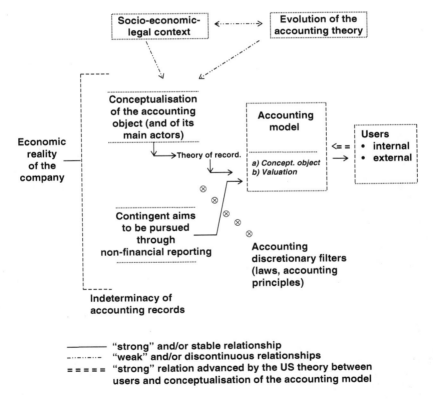

Figure 1.1 Zambon's original scheme (1996)

Source: Zambon, S. (1996). *Entità e proprietà nei bilanci di esercizio*. Padua: Cedam. (Entity and Proprietary in Financial Statements) as translated by the author.

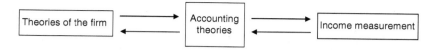

Figure 1.2 Logical correlation between theory of the firm, accounting theory and income measurement in financial reporting

Source: Presentation by Zambon, S. and Zan, L. at the European Accounting Association Conference, 1990, Budapest.

schemes to the concept of reporting boundaries, which is embedded in the conceptualisation of the object of the entity and, consequently, in that of the consolidated financial statement. Although it is possible to infer where the boundaries in the schemes lie, the works do not present any explicit *problematisation* of, and reflection on, the concept.

As for the notion of 'boundary transplantation', as advanced here, it has been adopted and articulated, especially in the legal field, in a comparative perspective. Indeed, the so-called 'legal transplant' has become crucial to the understanding of the processes through which law has been formed or transformed with the occurrence of globalisation, and Asian countries have offered cases for investigation in this respect (Gillespie, 2001; Harding, 2001; Sin and Roebuck, 1996; Xing, 2004). However, for the sake of the argument proposed here, it should be noted that within this field the concept of transplantation is often associated with the idea of policy borrowing from one jurisdiction to another. As mentioned by Alan Watson, who coined the term 'legal transplantation' in the 1970s and since then has been one of the principal proponents of the 'transplant theory' in the field of comparative law:

> [T]ransplanting is, in fact, the most fertile source of development. Most changes in most systems are the result of borrowing. [. . .] Since borrowing – often with modifications – is the main way in which the law of any Western system develops, at the centre of study of Comparative Law should be Legal Transplants.
>
> (Watson as cited by Ewald, 1995:498–499)

Although some authors have pointed out that there is a difference between these two terms, in that 'borrowing' implies a voluntary exchange between equals, to put it differently, a proximity, and that the borrowed good will be returned unmodified (Lane Scheppele as cited by Perju, 2012),[3] we will use them here interchangeably. Indeed, the investigation of whether the financial and non-financial are equivalent, adjacent realms, and the extent of it, is not at stake here, but it will be the focus of future related works.[4]

In addition to the above qualifications, it is observed that despite that the concepts of 'borrowing' and 'transplantation' could be conceived as similar to the ones of 'migration', 'expansion', 'creolisation' and 'hybridisation', they do present attributes which differentiate them quite sharply. Indeed, 'migration' describes

> all movements across systems, overt or covert, episodic or incremental, planned or evolved, initiated by the giver or receiver, accepted or rejected, adopted or adapted, concerned with substantive doctrine or with institutional design or some more abstract or intangible constitutional sensibility or ethos.
>
> (Walker, 2007:320–321)

'Expansion' entails the effort to "monopolize jurisdictional control over a disputed ontological domain by rival epistemic authorities" (Lamont and Molnar, 2002). In a similar vein, the processes of 'blending', 'creolisation' and 'hybridisation', which have been extensively used in relation to the dynamics of boundary change, refer to the creation of new distinct objects, identities and cultures by means of an assimilation of the features that belong to neighbouring cultures, disciplines or in general fields. They undermine the creation of new identities through a mixture.[5] On the one hand the adoption of a concept as 'migration' would appear too elastic, rendering it difficult to understand a process through which this passage occurs. On the other hand, the notion of 'expansion' is too rigid, being associated with the attempt of monopolisation. Furthermore, as compared to the other notions, despite a new 'identity' – in this case the definition and process of boundary setting for non-financial reporting – being created, its composing elements maintain their original attributes. They do not find themselves indigenised.

With regards to the notion of 'transplanting', even though it is used for the first time here in the context of setting the boundaries of reporting, it has previously been adopted in accounting research studies that have investigated the transnational phenomena. Chiapello and Medjad (2009), for example, adopt 'transplantation' to refer to the process through which IASB norms have been transplanted into EU law. In particular, they maintain that the ignorance of a border and the less branded nature of private standards can "facilitate their appropriation by local lawmakers and eventually, their transplantation in their respective domestic systems" (Chiapello and Medjad, 2009:455). Similarly, Rahaman (2010), in investigating the possibilities for critical research in Africa, and especially commenting on the wide adoption of Western accounting practices in the continent, equates the concept of transplantation to "blind imitations" (p. 421). Arya and Zhang (2009) acknowledge that the adoption of CSR initiatives by African corporations derives in many respects from a "transplant from the developed world" where they have been judged as acceptable (Arya and Zhang, 2009:5). Other works have used it, although without defining it. Bhimani (1993) refers to the "transplantation of notions of accountability and responsibility" (Bhimani, 1993:2), and Christensen (2011) maintains that in order to succeed in conducting analytical modelling there should be a "taking the real world setting and transplanting it into an abstract setting" (Christensen, 2011:46).

Notes

1 The expression 'reporting entity' refers to the scope of entities included in the preparation of financial or non-financial report. It can represent a single entity, such as a parent, or a group of entities – typically referred to a 'group' or 'economic entity'.
2 General system theory advanced in organisation already referred to this topic in the 1950s.
3 Different is the conceptualisation of 'boundaries borrowing' advanced by some sociologists according to whom it is one of the mechanisms of boundaries change or, in the extreme case, erosion, through which 'elements from the rival category' or, more simply, 'distinctions already visible' are copied or emulated and installed in a new location (Tilly, 2004). This way, boundaries are not invented and inequality is not intended to be created in a massive and durable way (ibid., p. 219).
4 Similarly, the concept of 'mimesis' (Girard, 1976) will be here conceived as the resulting effect of the 'transplantation process' and no further examination will be here advanced.
5 For a critical review of how the concept of creolisation has been (unreflexively) extrapolated and used in anthropology and in other disciplines see Palmié (2006). For the argument here at stake, its definition as the one proposed in the text is satisfactory.

Bibliography

Abbott, A. (1995), Things of boundaries, *Social Research*, 62(4), pp. 857–882.
Afuah, A. (2001), Dynamic boundaries of the firm: Are firms better off being vertically integrated in the face of a technological change? *Academy of Management Journal*, 44(6), pp. 1211–1228.
Anderson, G. (2010), Transfer of carbon liability under the proposed Carbon Pollution Reduction Scheme, *Monash University Law Review*, 36(1), p. 304.
Andrei, P. (2007), Area di riferimento del bilancio sociale [The scope of social reporting], in M. Andreaus (ed.), *La rendicontazione sociale nei gruppi aziendali* [Groups' social reporting], pp. 75–95 (Milan: McGraw-Hill).
Andrei, P., and Pesci, C. (2009), L'area di riferimento del bilancio socio-ambientale nei gruppi aziendali: spunti critici di riflessione emergenti da un'indagine empirica [The scope of social-environmental reporting within groups: Critical reflections from an empirical analysis], *Financial Reporting*, 1(2), pp. 45–70.
Annisette, M. (2017), Discourse of the professions: The making, normalizing and taming of Ontario's 'foreign-trained accountant', *Accounting, Organizations and Society*, 60, pp. 37–61.

Araujo, L., Dubois, A., and Gadde, L. E. (2003), The multiple boundaries of the firm, *Journal of Management Studies*, 40(5), pp. 1255–1277.

Archel, P., Fernández, M., and Larrinaga, C. (2008), The organizational and operational boundaries of triple bottom line reporting: A survey, *Environmental Management*, 41(1), pp. 106–117.

Ardemani, E. (1968), L'evoluzione del concetto di impresa e dei sistemi contabili in Italia [The evolution of firm concept and accounting systems in Italy], *Rivista dei dottori commercialisti*, 3(May–June), pp. 411–430.

Arya, B., and Zhang, G. (2009), Institutional reforms and investor reactions to CSR announcements: Evidence from an emerging economy, *Journal of Management Studies*, 46(7), pp. 1089–1112.

Barth, F. (1969), *Ethnic groups and boundaries: The social organization of culture differences* (New York: Little, Brown).

Baxter, W. (1984), *Inflation accounting* (Oxford: Philip Allan).

Bensadon, D. (2005), La frontière comptable de l'entité groupe: évolution du concept de périmètre de consolidation des comptes du milieu des années 1960 à la loi du 3 janvier 1985 [The accounting frontier of the group entity: Evolution of the consolidation scope concept from the mid-1960s to the law of 3 January 1985], *Entreprises et histoire*, 2, pp. 8–22.

Bhimani, A. (1993), Indeterminacy and the specificity of accounting change: Renault 1898–1938, *Accounting, Organizations and Society*, 18(1), pp. 1–39.

Biondi, Y., Canziani, A., and Kirat, T. (2008), *The firm as an entity: Implications for economics, accounting and the law* (London and New York: Routledge).

Biondi, Y., and Zambon, S. (2013), *Accounting and business economics: Insights from national traditions* (London and New York: Routledge).

Bontis, N., and Fitz-Enz, J. (2002), Intellectual capital ROI: A causal map of human capital antecedents and consequents, *Journal of Intellectual Capital*, 3(3), pp. 223–247.

Bourdieu, P. (1975), The specificity of the scientific field and the social conditions of the progress of reason, *Information (International Social Science Council)*, 14(6), pp. 19–47.

Brusoni, S., Prencipe, A., and Pavitt, K. (2001), Knowledge specialisation, organisational coupling and the boundaries of the firm: Why do firms know more than they do? *Administrative Science Quarterly*, 46(4), pp. 597–621.

Carlile, P. R. (2002), A pragmatic view of knowledge and boundaries: Boundary objects in new product development, *Organization Science*, 13(4), pp. 442–455.

Chandler, A. D. (1992), What is a firm – A historical perspective, *European Economic Review*, 36(2–3), pp. 483–492.

Chiapello, E., and Medjad, K. (2009), An unprecedented privatisation of mandatory standard-setting: The case of European accounting policy, *Critical Perspectives on Accounting*, 20(4), pp. 448–468.

Choudhry, S. (2007), *The migration of constitutional ideas* (Cambridge: Cambridge University Press).

Christensen, J. (2011), Good analytical research, *European Accounting Review*, 20(1), pp. 41–51.

Coase, R. H. (1937), The nature of the firm. *Economica*, 4(16), pp. 386–405.

Dosi, G., and Teece, D. J. (1998), Organizational competencies and the boundaries of the firm, in *Markets and organization*, pp. 281–302 (Berlin and Heidelberg: Springer).

Durkheim, E. (1911), *Les formes élementaires de la vie religieuse* (Paris: Alcan) [1965. *The elementary forms of religious life*. New York: Free Press].
Edwards, P., Birkin, F. K., and Woodward, D. G. (1999), Extending the boundaries of annual reporting: A challenge to the accountant and her profession, *Journal of Applied Accounting Research*, 5(1), pp. 37–67.
Epstein, C. F. (1992), Tinker-bells and pinups: The construction and reconstruction of gender boundaries at work, in M. Lamont and M. Fournier (eds.), *Cultivating differences: Symbolic boundaries and the making of inequality* (Chicago: University of Chicago Press).
Evans, L. (2004), Language, translation and the problem of international accounting communication, *Accounting, Auditing & Accountability Journal*, 17(2), pp. 210–248.
Evans, L. (2010), Observations on the changing language of accounting, *Accounting History*, 15(4), pp. 439–462.
Ewald, W. (1995), Comparative jurisprudence (II): The logic of legal transplants, *The American Journal of Comparative Law*, 43(4), pp. 489–510.
Foucault, M. (1970), *The order of things: An archaeology of knowledge* (New York: Pantheon).
Foucault, M. (1972), *The archeology of knowledge* (New York: Pantheon).
Fuller, S. (1991), Disciplinary boundaries and the rhetoric of the social sciences, *Poetics Today*, 12(2), pp. 301–325.
Giannessi, E. (1969), Considerazioni critiche intorno al concetto di azienda [Some critical considerations on the concept of azienda], in VV.AA., *Scritti in onore di Giordano Dell'Amore. Saggi di discipline aziendali e sociali* [Writings in honor of Giordano Dell'Amore: Essays on business and social disciplines], Vol. 1, pp. 461–588 (Milan: Giuffrè).
Gieryn, T. F. (1983), Boundary-work and the demarcation of science from non-science: Strains and interests in professional ideologies of scientists, *American Sociological Review*, pp. 781–795.
Gillespie, J. (2001), Globalisation and legal transplantation: Lessons from the past, *Deakin Law Review*, 6, p. 286.
Girard, R. (1976), *Deceit, desire, and the novel: Self and other in literary structure* (Baltimore, MD: Johns Hopkins University Press).
Gowthorpe, C. (2009), Wider still and wider? A critical discussion of intellectual capital recognition, measurement and control in a boundary theoretical context, *Critical Perspectives on Accounting*, 20(7), pp. 823–834.
Grandori, A. (2000), *Organisation and economic behaviour* (London and New York: Routledge).
Grossman, S., and Hart, O. (1986), The costs and benefits of integration: A theory of vertical and lateral integration, *Journal of Political Economy*, 94(4), pp. 691–719.
Gulbenkian Commission on the Restructuring of the Social Sciences (1996), *Open the social sciences: Report of the Gulbenkian Commission on the restructuring of the social sciences* (Stanford: Stanford University Press).
Harding, A. (2001), Comparative law and legal transplantation in South East Asia: Making sense of the 'Nomic Din', in D. Nelken and J. Feest (eds.), *Adapting legal cultures*, pp. 199–222 (London: Bloomsbury Publishing).
Haugen, E. (1950), The analysis of linguistic borrowing, *Language*, 26(2), pp. 210–231.

Heracleous, L. (2004), Boundaries in the study of organization, *Human Relations*, 57(1), pp. 95–103.
Hirschhorn, L., and Gilmore, T. (1992), The new boundaries of the 'boundaryless' company, *Harvard Business Review*, 70(3), pp. 104–115.
Horwitz, M. J. (2009), Constitutional transplants, *Theoretical Inquiries in Law*, 10(2), pp. 535–560.
Jacobides, M. G., and Billinger, S. (2006), Designing the boundaries of the firm: From 'make, buy, or ally' to the dynamic benefits of vertical architecture, *Organization Science*, 17(2), pp. 249–261.
Journet, D. (1993), Interdisciplinary discourse and 'boundary rhetoric' the case of SE Jelliffe, *Written Communication*, 10(4), pp. 510–541.
Kaboolian, L. (1998), The new public management: Challenging the boundaries of the management vs. administration debate, *Public Administration Review*, 58(3), pp. 189–193.
Kaspersen, M. (2013), *The construction of social and environmental reporting*, PhD School of Economics and Management, Copenhagen Business School.
Kettl, D. F. (2006), Managing boundaries in American administration: The collaboration imperative, *Public Administration Review*, 66(1), pp. 10–19.
Lamberton, G. (2005), Sustainability accounting – A brief history and conceptual framework, *Accounting Forum*, 29(1), pp. 7–26.
Lamont, M., and Molnár, V. (2002), The study of boundaries in the social sciences, *Annual Review of Sociology*, 28(1), pp. 167–195.
Lefebvre, C., and Lin, L. Q. (1991), On the scope of consolidation: A comparative study of the EEC 7th Directive, IAS 27 and the Belgian Royal Decree on Consolidation, *The British Accounting Review*, 23(2), pp. 133–147.
Leiblein, M. J., and Miller, D. J. (2003), An empirical examination of transaction- and firm-level influences on the vertical boundaries of the firm, *Strategic Management Journal*, 24(9), pp. 839–859.
Lev, B., and Zarowin, P. (1999), The boundaries of financial reporting and how to extend them, *Journal of Accounting Research*, 37(2), pp. 353–385.
Lightfoot, K. G., and Martinez, A. (1995), Frontiers and boundaries in archaeological perspective, *Annual Review of Anthropology*, 24(1), pp. 471–492.
Llewellyn, S. (1994), Managing the boundary: How accounting is implicated in maintaining the organization, *Accounting, Auditing & Accountability Journal*, 7(4), pp. 4–23.
Loasby, B. J. (1998a), The organisation of capabilities, *Journal of Economic Behavior & Organization*, 35(2), pp. 139–160.
Loasby, B. J. (1998b), The concept of capabilities, in N. J. Foss and B. J. Loasby (eds.), *Economic organization, capabilities and co-ordination: Essays in honour of G. B. Richardson*, pp. 163–182 (London: Routledge).
Marx, K. (1963), *The eighteenth Brumaire of Louis Napoleon* (New York: International Publishers).
Massey, D. (1999), Negotiating disciplinary boundaries, *Current Sociology*, 47(4), pp. 5–12.
Meyssonnier, F., and Pourtier, F. (2013), Contrôle du périmètre et périmètre de contrôle – Réflexion sur le système d'information comptable des groups, *Comptabilité-Contrôle-Audit*, 19(3), pp. 117–146.

Miller, P. (1998), The margins of accounting, *The Sociological Review*, 46(1), pp. 174–193.
Moneva, J. M., Archel, P., and Correa, C. (2006, June), GRI and the camouflaging of corporate unsustainability, *Accounting Forum*, 30(2), pp. 121–137.
Mouritsen, J., Larsen, H. T., and Bukh, P. N. (2001), Valuing the future: Intellectual capital supplements at Skandia, *Accounting, Auditing & Accountability Journal*, 14(4), pp. 399–422.
Musolf, L. D., and Seidman, H. (1980), The blurred boundaries of public administration, *Public Administration Review*, pp. 124–130.
Nelson, R., and Winter, S. G. (1982), *An evolutionary theory of economic change* (Cambridge: Harvard Business School Press).
Nelson, T., Wood, E., Hunt, J., and Thurbon, C. (2011), Improving Australian greenhouse gas reporting and financial analysis of carbon risk associated with investments, *Sustainability Accounting, Management and Policy Journal*, 2(1), pp. 147–157.
Nobes, C. (2002), An analysis of the international development of the equity method, *Abacus*, 38(1), pp. 16–45.
Nobes, C. (2014), The development of national and transnational regulation on the scope of consolidation, *Accounting, Auditing & Accountability Journal*, 27(6), pp. 995–1025.
Palmié, S. (2006), Creolization and its discontents, *Annual Review of Anthropology*, 35, pp. 433–456.
Penrose, E. (1959), *The theory of the growth of the firm* (Oxford: Basil Blackwell).
Perju, V. (2012), *Constitutional transplants, borrowing, and migrations*, Boston College Law School Faculty Papers.
Pesci, C., and Andrei, P. (2011), An empirical investigation into the boundary of corporate social reports and consolidated financial statements, *Social and Environmental Accountability Journal*, 31(1), pp. 73–84.
Pisano, G. P. (1990), The R&D boundaries of the firm: An empirical analysis, *Administrative Science Quarterly*, pp. 153–176.
Popper, K. (1957), *The poverty of historicism* (New York: Harper and Row).
Prahalad, C. K., and Hamel, G. (1990), The core competence of the corporation, *Harvard Business Review* (May–June), pp. 1–15.
Rahaman, A. S. (2010), Critical accounting research in Africa: Whence and whither, *Critical Perspectives on Accounting*, 21(5), pp. 420–427.
Rao, H., Monin, P., and Durand, R. (2005), Border crossing: Bricolage and the erosion of categorical boundaries in French gastronomy, *American Sociological Review*, 70(6), pp. 968–991.
Richardson, G. B. (1972), The organisation of industry, *The Economic Journal*, 82(September), pp. 883–896.
Richardson, G. B. (1998), Some principles of economic organization, in N. J. Foss and B. J. Loasby (eds.), *Economic organization, capabilities and co-ordination: Essays in honour of G. B. Richardson*, pp. 44–62 (London: Routledge).
Roos, J. (1998), Exploring the concept of intellectual capital (IC), *Long Range Planning*, 31(1), pp. 150–153.
Saccon, C. (2008), Perimeter of consolidation: Converging regulations and national effects, *Revista Economica*, 40(3), pp. 75–88.

Santos, F. M., and Eisenhardt, K. M. (2005), Organizational boundaries and theories of organization, *Organization Science*, 16(5), pp. 491–508.

Sin, K. K., and Roebuck, D. (1996), Language engineering for legal transplantation: Conceptual problems in creating common law Chinese, *Language & Communication*, 16(3), pp. 235–254.

Solomons, D. (1978), The politicization of accounting, *Journal of Accountancy (pre-1986)*, 146(5), p. 65.

Sprague, Ch. E. (1907), *The philosophy of accounts* (New York: Published by the author).

Star, S. L. (1988), The structure of ill-structured solutions: Boundary objects and heterogeneous distributed problem solving, in *Readings in distributed artificial intelligence*, pp. 37–54 (San Francisco: Morgan Kaufman).

Teece, D. J., and Pisano, G. (1994), The dynamic capabilities of firms: An introduction, *Industrial and Corporate Change*, 3(3), pp. 537–556.

Teece, D. J., Pisano, G., and Shuen, A. (1997), Dynamic capabilities and strategic management, *Strategic Management Journal*, pp. 509–533.

Tilly, C. (2004), Social boundary mechanisms, *Philosophy of the Social Sciences*, 34(2), pp. 211–236.

Viganò, E. (1966, January–April), L''entity concept' nella dottrina contabile americana [The 'entity concept' in the American accounting doctrine], *Studi Economici*, 1–2, pp. 107–146.

Walker, N. (2007), The migration of constitutional ideas and the migration of the constitutional idea: The case of the EU, in S. Choudhry (ed.), *The migration of constitutional ideas*, pp. 316–343 (Cambridge: Cambridge University Press).

Walker, R. G. (1978), International accounting compromises: The case of consolidation accounting, *Abacus*, 14(2), pp. 97–111.

Wallerstein, I. (1995), What are we bounding, and whom, when we bound social research, *Social Research*, 62(4), pp. 839–856.

Walton, P. (2006), A research note: Fair value and executory contracts: Moving the boundaries in international financial reporting, *Accounting and Business Research*, 36(4), pp. 337–343.

Weber, M. (1978), *Economy and society*, Vol. 1 (Berkeley: University of California Press).

Williamson, O. E. (1975), *Markets and hierarchies: Analysis and antitrust implications* (New York: Free Press).

Xing, L. (2004), Some new insights into legal transplantation: From 'history' to 'present', *Social Sciences in China*, 5, p. 1.

Young, A. (2010), Greenhouse gas accounting: Global problem, national policy, local fugitives, *Sustainability Accounting, Management and Policy Journal*, 1(1), pp. 89–95.

Zambon, S. (1996), *Entità e proprietà nei bilanci di esercizio* [Entity and proprietary in financial statements] (Padua: Cedam).

Zambon, S., and Zan, L. (2000), Accounting relativism: The unstable relationship between income measurement and theories of the firm, *Accounting, Organizations and Society*, 25(8), pp. 799–822.

Zan, L. (1990), *Economia dell'impresa cooperativa* [The economics of the co-operative society] (Turin: Utet).

Zappa, G. (1957), *Le produzioni nell'economia delle imprese* [The production activities in the economy] (Milan: Giuffre).

Zeff, S. A. (1978), *A critical examination of the orientation postulate in accounting* (New York: Arno Press – orig. ed., 1961, University of Michigan).

Zimmerman, B. J., and Hurst, D. K. (1993), Breaking the boundaries: The fractal organization, *Journal of Management Inquiry*, 2(4), pp. 334–355.

2 Boundaries in financial reporting

As previously explained, the definition of reporting boundaries represents a critical aspect for conceptualising the theory of the firm. It sets the logic of what is included (and excluded) from reporting in reflecting the performance and viability of the reporting entity's business model that standard setters and frameworks attempt to standardise. Indeed, the definition of boundaries is directly linked to what is conceived as being an entity and to its objective. Accordingly, it can be said that it embodies the focal aspect that allows an understanding of the ways through which value is created. Following this line of thought, this Chapter will review the ways in which reporting boundaries have been defined with reference to financial (both company and group) reporting, outlining the fundamental theories that underlie the different approaches, the views put forth by the key standard setters, namely the International Accounting Standards Board (IASB) and the Financial Accounting Standards Board (FASB) on consolidation and on the principal technical and measurement implications that derive from them, such as the treatment of special purpose entities and of non-controlling (minority) interests.

2.1 Proprietary vs. entity theories

In the context of financial reporting, and especially of external reporting by large listed entities, it is important to note that where the reporting boundary lies with respect to the value creation process is not clear cut. Indeed, the problem of where the value creation process of the organisation 'ends' is not necessarily seen as a source of the principal characteristic of financial reporting. Accordingly, the definition in these frameworks is not embedded within any specific economic theories but can be conceptualised in relation to those features that are central to the existence of the organisation, such as the capital it draws upon in order to conduct its activity, the relationships it enters with those actors that surround it and the ways surplus/value is defined and measured. In this respect, it is possible to delineate a 'proprietary' view (Hatfield, 1909; Kester, 1917–1918; Sprague, 1907) of financial reporting. According to this view, the resources are owned by the organisation, and the main actors that surround its activities, and hence those that represent the main target for surplus distribution (defined as proprietor's net worth or net profit) are shareholders or equity bearers. The relationships undertaken with the latter do not give rise to a cost or liability. A distinction has however to be made. Where the 'proprietary' view is applied to a single company, the equity bearers correspond to the proprietors. Otherwise, in the case of a group, the equity bearers correspond to the controlling company which has a dominant influence on the other companies of the group. An evolution of this perspective is the 'entity view' (Paton, 1922). According to this perspective, the resources are not necessarily 'owned' but controlled by the organisation and the focus is on the future economic benefits that are expected (e.g. in the case of leasing). To put it differently, the firm is conceived as being distinct from its proprietors. In establishing relations with the actors, the economic entity is seen as prominent vis-à-vis all stakeholders and the distribution of any surplus to shareholders may be treated as a cost (rather than a return on capital) according to the approach adopted ('distributional' according to Paton, 1922; or 'institutional' according to Anthony, 1975; Li, 1960a, 1960b; Staubus, 1959). Indeed, in the former case, surplus is calculated as the sum of profit, interests on long-term debt and taxes. In the latter two approaches, dividends or cost of equity capital are subtracted from profit. This way, surplus is defined as 'net profit to the entity'.

A third perspective for defining reporting boundaries with reference to individual company reporting can be identified in the so-called 'enterprise/institutional theory' proposed by scholars such as Suojanen (1954) and Ardemani (1968). According to them, the company is conceived as a coalition of resources belonging to various stakeholders and the relationships undertaken with them are determined at no cost. With reference to the definition of surplus, Suojanen originated the concept of 'value added', broadly conceived as the measurement of the flow of output and its division amongst participants in the organisation.

Despite these advances in the initial conceptualisation of how reporting boundaries are defined, this perspective has been rejected with the rise of group financial reporting (also known as consolidated accounts), embedding a neo-classical view of the firm. Indeed, it is precisely when value is created not only by a single company but as a group of companies that the understanding of what effectively contributes to this process becomes significant. In this respect, probably the most familiar and pioneering work was that by Moonitz regarding the application of entity theory (1942, 1951) to consolidated accounts. According to Moonitz, "a group of closely allied corporations (should be conceived) as a distinct economic or accounting entity, despite the existence of legal lines of separation among the constituent parts" (Moonitz, 1942:vii). The criteria through which it is possible to define the scope of consolidation relies on the concept of control, in particular *actual control*, that is through voting rights, and *de facto control*, without voting rights. The manner through which surplus is calculated mirrors this conception and, therefore, profit (flow) and equity (stock) are measured from the perspective of the economic entity conceived as a whole. This theory has overtaken the so-called proprietary view, which had previously dominated accounting theory where transactions and financial reporting are analysed and prepared from the lens of the proprietor(s) (Kell, 1953). The main criterion for determining the scope of consolidation passed from the presence of voting rights and 'ownership', to one based on control or dominant influence – via voting rights or other legal arrangements – and thus to the most recent and blurred one of 'power'. In a similar vein, the calculation of surplus strictly reflects the evolution of this theory, from the narrowly conceived proprietary view which sees profit as measured based on the proportional consolidation method, to the parent company theory wherein profit and equity are measured from the majority interests perspective.

2.2 The IASB and FASB views

Since the proprietary and entity perspectives[1] have been advanced, the problem of how to identify and define the boundaries of reporting has not been comprehensively addressed from an institutional perspective until the beginning of the 1960s in the US and of the 1980s in continental Europe, when the first developments towards the elaboration and diffusion of international accounting standards occurred. One of the initial principal documents that was released in this respect was the EC 7th Accounting Council Directive of 13 June 1983, which states that the determinants for requiring a company to prepare consolidated accounts are based on the majority of voting rights, the right to appoint or remove a majority of the members of the administrative, management or supervisory body of another company and is at the same time a shareholder in or member of that company, or to the exercise of a dominant or significant influence (which refers to the 20% or more of the shareholders' or members' voting rights in the company). However, a relevant exception is related to those companies whose activities are different from the one of the controlling company. As pointed out in the Directive:

> Where the activities of one or more undertakings to be consolidated are so different that their inclusion in the consolidated accounts would be incompatible with the obligation imposed in Article 16 (3), such

undertakings must, without prejudice to Article 33 of this Directive, be excluded from the consolidation.

(EC 7th Accounting Council Directive: Article 14, 1)[2]

Drawing on this logic, in 1989 IASC developed IAS 27 *Consolidated Financial Statements and Accounting for Investments in Subsidiaries*. Under IAS 27, as re-issued in 2008, the basis of consolidation shifted to the concept of 'control' which was defined as "the power to govern the financial and operating policies of an entity so as to obtain benefits from its activities" and in particular,

> control is presumed to exist when the parent owns directly, or indirectly through subsidiaries, more than half of the voting rights of the entity. (...) Control also exists even when the parent owns one half or less of the voting power of an entity when there is:
>
> - Power over more than one half of the voting rights by virtue of an agreement with other investors, or
> - Power to govern the financial and operating policies of the entity under a statute or an agreement; or
> - Power to appoint or remove the majority of the members of the board of directors or equivalent governing body and control of the entity is by that board or body; or
> - Power to cast the majority of votes at a meeting of the board of directors or equivalent governing body and control of the entity is by that board or body.
>
> (IAS 27:13)

In terms of treatment of intercompany transactions, IAS 27 (as revised in 2008) prescribed that intragroup balances, transactions, income, and expenses should be eliminated in full. In addition, it was indicated that "Intragroup losses may indicate that an impairment loss on the related asset should be recognised [IAS 27.24–25]. The financial statements of the parent and its subsidiaries used in preparing the consolidated financial statements should all be prepared as of the same reporting date, unless it is impracticable to do so" [IAS 27.26].

In IFRS 10 *Consolidated Financial Statements*, which replaced IAS 27 in May 2011 with effect from annual periods beginning on or after 1 January 2013, the concept of *control* has been linked much more to the one of *power* and the possibility to use it, even if it is not clear whether power should be actually exercised or only nominal/potential. In addition, as compared to the definition advanced in IAS 27, there is an explicit reference to the relation between power and returns:

An investor controls an investee when the investor is exposed, or has rights, to variable returns from its involvement with the investee and has the ability to affect those returns through its power over the investee.

(IFRS 10:5–6; IFRS 10:8)

An investor controls an investee if and only if the investor has all of the following elements (IFRS 10:7):

- power over the investee, i.e. the investor has existing rights that give it the ability to direct the relevant activities (the activities that significantly affect the investee's returns);
- exposure, or rights, to variable returns from its involvement with the investee;
- the ability to use its power over the investee to affect the amount of the investor's returns.

Power arises from rights. Such rights can be straightforward (e.g. through voting rights) or be complex (e.g. embedded in contractual arrangements). An investor that holds only protective rights cannot have power over an investee and so cannot control an investee.

(IFRS 10:11, IFRS 10:14)

A particular specification refers to the definition of power, in that it refers to those existing rights that give the current ability to direct the relevant activities, where relevant activities designates those that significantly affect the investee's returns (IFRS 10: Appendix A).

Whilst IAS 27 required the inclusion of potential voting rights in the assessment of control only if currently exercisable, IFRS 10 requires them to be included if they are substantive. Another difference between the two standards refers to the guidance that IFRS provides for those situations where a 'de facto power' exists, that is when an investor has sufficient rights to have power, even though it has less than 50% of the voting rights. In this case, it indicates that sufficient rights arise from an investor's voting rights, contractual agreements with other vote holders, other contractual arrangements, potential voting rights or a combination of these.

As for the treatment of intercompany transactions, it is prescribed that in preparing consolidated financial statements, companies should:

a) combine like items of assets, liabilities, equity, income, expenses and cash flows of the parent with those of its subsidiaries;

b) offset (eliminate) the carrying amount of the parent's investment in each subsidiary and the parent's portion of equity of each subsidiary (IFRS 3 explains how to account for any related goodwill);
c) eliminate in full intragroup assets and liabilities, equity, income, expenses and cash flows relating to transactions between entities of the group (profits or losses resulting from intragroup transactions that are recognised in assets, such as inventory and fixed assets, are eliminated in full).

However, these standards refer to a parent entity and its ability to exercise control over another entity (or groups of entities). In the case of two or more parties that jointly control an entity, IFRS 11 and IFRS 12^3 apply. According to the former, which applies to joint arrangements since 2011 (when it replaced IAS 31), "(joint) control is the contractually agreed sharing of control of an arrangement, which exists only when decisions about the relevant activities require the unanimous consent of the parties sharing control" (IFRS 11:7). "The requirement for unanimous consent means that any party with joint control of the arrangement can prevent any of the other parties, or a group of the parties, from making unilateral decisions (about the relevant activities) without its consent" (IFRS 11:B9). This definition applies to two types of arrangements, that are joint operations – whereby the parties that have joint control of the arrangement *have rights to the assets, and obligations for the liabilities, relating to the arrangement* (IFRS 11:15, emphasis added) – or joint ventures – whereby the parties that have joint control of the arrangement *have rights to the net assets of the arrangement* (IFRS 11: Appendix A, emphasis added).

The definition of significant influence is provided in IAS 28 *Investments in Associates and Joint Ventures*, which regulates how to apply the equity method to investments in associates and joint ventures. In particular, in this standard 'associate' is defined through the concept of significant influence, being:

> Where an entity holds 20% or more of the voting power (directly or through subsidiaries) on an investee, it will be presumed the investor has significant influence unless it can be clearly demonstrated that this is not the case. If the holding is less than 20%, the entity will be presumed not to have significant influence unless such influence can be clearly demonstrated. A substantial or majority ownership by another investor does not necessarily preclude an entity from having significant influence.
>
> (IAS 28:5)

The existence of significant influence by an entity is usually evidenced in one or more of the following ways (IAS 28:6):

- representation on the board of directors or equivalent governing body of the investee;
- participation in the policy-making process, including participation in decisions about dividends or other distributions;
- material transactions between the entity and the investee;
- interchange of managerial personnel; or
- provision of essential technical information.

In order to depict the intertwinements between these accounting standards, IASB has released a scheme aimed to clarify where and when these definitions have to be employed (Figure 2.1).

More recently, Directive 2013/34/EU of the European Parliament and of the Council of 26 June 2013 may be said to have not substantially changed this approach (Alexander, 2015).

As for business combinations, the first standard issued by IASB in 1983 related to business combinations was IAS 22. In terms of consolidation procedures, two options were available – the 'pooling-of-interests' and the 'purchase method'. The first option was applied in case of uniting of interests. Under it:

> financial statement items of uniting entities should be combined, in both the current and prior periods, as if they had been united from the beginning

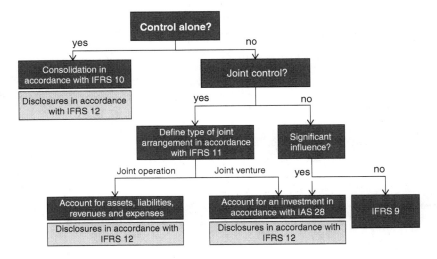

Figure 2.1 Interactions between IFRS 10, 11, 12 and IAS 28

of the earliest period presented [IAS 22:78]; any difference between the amount recorded as share capital issued plus any additional consideration in the form of cash or other assets and the amount recorded for the share capital acquired should be adjusted against equity [IAS 22:79] and the costs of the combination should be expensed when incurred [IAS 22:82].

For acquisitions, the purchase method should be used. It prescribed that "the income statement should incorporate the results of the acquiree from the date of acquisition and the balance sheet should include the identifiable assets and liabilities of the acquiree and any goodwill or negative goodwill arising" [IAS 22:19]. In 2004, IFRS 3 was issued, superseding IAS 22. This standard eliminated the 'pooling-of-interests' method and indicated the 'purchase method' as the only applicable method. In the revised IFRS 3 (2008), the acquisition method (previously called the 'purchase method' in the 2004 version of the standard) is now applied. According to this, the identifiable assets acquired, liabilities assumed, and non-controlling interests in the acquiree, are recognised separately from goodwill [IFRS 3:10] and all assets acquired and liabilities assumed in a business combination are measured at acquisition-date fair value [IFRS 3:18]. For the measurement of NCI, two options are available on a transaction-by-transaction basis as illustrated in the following sections.

Compared to IASB, the evolution of the FASB (and its predecessors) rules for consolidating financial statements appears less scattered. The main pronouncements and statements issued in order to regulate the consolidation procedure can be traced to two main sources, the Accounting Research Bulletin (ARB) 51 *Consolidated Financial Statements* adopted in 1959 by the Committee on Accounting Procedure of the AICPA, and the Accounting Principles Board (APB) Opinion No. 16 *Business Combinations* (1970) (which has been superseded by Financial Accounting Statement no. 141 *Business Combinations* in 2001, revised in 2007). According to Accounting Research Bulletin 51, the determinant for consolidation did not differ considerably from IAS 27 (2008), as it relied on the existence of a 'control of financial interest' based on the ownership of over 50% of the voting shares. As the Bulletin states:

> The usual condition for a controlling financial interest is *ownership of a majority voting interest, and, therefore, as a general rule ownership by one company, directly or indirectly, of over fifty percent of the outstanding voting shares of another company is a condition pointing toward consolidation.*
>
> (ARB 51, 1959: para. 1, emphasis added)

However, a few, but nevertheless relevant, exceptions were present to this general rule (in paras 2 and 3). One referred to situations "where control is likely to be temporary, or where it does not rest with the majority owners" and to subsidiaries that had a relative large minority interest or that are foreign subsidiaries (ARB 51, 1959: para. 2). The second exception, which had a greater impact on consolidation practice, related to the group of companies that is heterogeneous in character, sometimes referred to as the 'non-heterogeneous' exception. Similar to the EC 7th Accounting Directive, it clearly prescribed that in those cases where the presentation of separated or combined statements "would be more informative to shareholders and creditors of the parent company than would be the inclusion of such subsidiaries in the consolidation" (para. 3) i.e. these companies were allowed to present separate or combined statements, and thus could avoid consolidation. This was the main practice followed until the release of Statement of Financial Accounting Standards No. 94 by FASB in 1987. This standard eliminated the 'non-heterogeneous' exception as well as the relatively large minority interests exception and other restrictive policies. Accordingly, ARB 51 as amended by SFAS No. 94 reads:

> The usual condition for a controlling financial interest is ownership of a majority voting interest, and, therefore, as a general rule ownership by one company, directly or indirectly, of over fifty percent of the outstanding voting shares of another company is a condition pointing toward consolidation. However, there are exceptions to this general rule. A majority-owned subsidiary shall not be consolidated if control does not rest with the majority owner (as, for instance, if the subsidiary is in legal reorganization or in bankruptcy or operates under foreign exchange restrictions, controls, or other governmentally imposed uncertainties so severe that they cast significant doubt on the parent's ability to control the subsidiary).
>
> (para. 2)

As for the treatment of intercompany balances (consolidation procedure) and the treatment of minority interests it was indicated that:

> In the preparation of consolidated statements, *intercompany balances and transactions should be eliminated.* [. . .] As consolidated statements are based on the assumption that they represent the financial position and operating results of a single business enterprise, such statements should not include gain or loss on transactions among the companies in the group. Accordingly, *any intercompany profit or loss on assets remaining within the group should be eliminated*; the concept usually applied for this purpose is gross profit or loss.
>
> (ARB 51, 1959: paras. 2;6, emphasis added)

With reference to minority interests it was stated that:

> The amount of intercompany profit or loss to be eliminated in accordance with paragraph 6 is not affected by the existence of a minority interest. [...] The elimination of the intercompany profit or loss may be allocated proportionately between the majority and minority interests.
> (ARB 51, 1959: para. 14)

However, as opposed to IASB and the path it has taken towards the introduction of more broad concepts, such as the one of 'power', FASB has assumed a different approach in developing these standards. The release of FAS no. 160, introduced no modifications with reference to the general consolidation procedures. Control of financial interest, i.e. the ownership of the majority of voting shares, is still the condition required for consolidating. The only amendments to consolidation procedures have been made to render it consistent with FAS 141(R) *Business Combinations*. Furthermore, as illustrated in the following section, substantial changes have been made referring to the displacement and measurement of minority interests.

The same cannot be said with reference to business combinations. Indeed, the fundamental amendment to APB Opinion No. 16 by FAS 141 related to the use of a single-method approach, being the purchase method. However, no considerable changes were made to the provisions related to the application of this method.

Under FAS 141(R) (2007), which replaced FAS 141, the requirement to use the purchase method (which the new standard re-named the acquisition method) was retained, even though FAS 141(R) defined what is an acquirer and when the acquisition date is to be established. This way, with the release of FAS 141(R) all identifiable assets acquired, all liabilities assumed, and any non-controlling interest in the acquiree must be generally measured at fair value *as of the acquisition date*. This replaced the cost-allocation process of FAS 141, according to which the acquirer allocates the cost of the target institution to the identifiable assets acquired and liabilities assumed based in most cases on their estimated fair values at the date of the acquisition.

2.3 Some technical and measurement implications

2.3.1 *The case of special purpose entities*

Another topic that it is worth considering in the investigation of reporting boundaries refers to special purpose entities (or vehicles). Probably the most well-known case is the one of Enron, a US energy corporation, which used this type of entity to manipulate financial statements during the late 1990s and the early 2000s.

After the infamous collapse of the company, both IASB and FASB started to pay more attention to this type of entity and advanced standards in order to regulate them. With reference to IASB, special purpose entities were regulated by IAS 27 in conjunction with SIC – 12 *Special Purpose Entities*.

Under SIC-12, an entity must consolidate a special purpose entity when, in substance, the entity controls the special purpose entity. In particular, SIC-12 set out the circumstances that identify control as follows:

(a) the activities of the acquiree are conducted on behalf of the entity according to its specific business needs so that the entity obtains benefits from the acquiree's operations;
(b) the entity has the decision-making powers to obtain the majority of benefits or has delegated those powers through an 'autopilot' mechanism;
(c) the entity has rights to obtain the majority of benefits and, therefore, may be exposed to risks from the acquiree's activities; or
(d) the entity retains the majority of residual or ownership risks related to the acquiree or its assets in order to obtain benefits from its activities.

[SIC-12.10]

For periods beginning on or after 1 January 2013, IFRS 10 Consolidated Financial Statements superseded IAS 27 and SIC 12. As compared to IAS 27 and SIC-12, IFRS 10 requires that, in order for an investor with decision-making rights to have control, it must act as a principal and not an agent, that is it may delegate decision-making rights to another party on some specific issues or on all relevant activities.

Under US GAAP, this type of entity was officially regulated only recently with the issuance by FASB of the Interpretation (FIN) No. 46 in January 2003, which was replaced by (FIN) No. 46R in December of the same year. Prior to these pronouncements, the occurrence of certain criteria to be met determined the consolidation (or not) of these entities and were based on the consolidation procedures of ARB No. 51 which, as previously described, presumed the existence of the control of financial interests.

According to (FIN) No. 46R a 'variable interest entity' (which was substituted for the previously adopted term 'special purpose entity') represents an entity that is "not self-supporting in that it cannot finance its activities without receiving additional subordinated financial support from another entity (the so-called primary beneficiary) or individual".

If the primary beneficiary is an entity, the variable interest entity will be consolidated if three criteria are met, specifically:

- There must be a variable interest entity, that is (a) the total equity investment at risk is not sufficient to permit it to finance its activities

without obtaining additional subordinated financial support provided by any parties (e.g. individual or entity), including equity holders or (b) as a group, the holders of equity investments at risk lack any one of three characteristics that are typical of a controlling financial interest, i.e. they lack the direct or indirect ability (through voting rights or similar rights) to make decisions about the entity's activities that have a significant effect on the success of the entity; they have no obligation to absorb the expected losses of the entity; they have no right to receive the expected residual returns of the entity).
- Entities and/or individuals must have variable interests in the variable interest entity.
- An entity or individual must be the primary beneficiary of the variable interest entity; the one that gives the majority.

The consolidation procedure of a variable interest entity reflects that its assets, liabilities, and non-controlling (minority) interests should be recorded at fair value by the primary beneficiary at the date the entity becomes the primary beneficiary.

SFAS 167, issued in June 2009, revised (FN) 46R. Under the new Standard, the notion of primary beneficiary substantially changed. Indeed, an enterprise is identified as primary beneficiary if it consolidates a variable interest entity. Consolidation occurs when the primary beneficiary has a variable interest (or combination of variable interests) that provides the enterprise with a controlling financial interest. Controlling financial interest in a variable interest entity occurs if the enterprise has both of the following characteristics:

- the power to direct the activities of a variable interest entity that most significantly impact the entity's economic performance;
- the obligation to absorb losses of the entity that could potentially be significant to the variable interest entity or the right to receive benefits from the entity that could potentially be significant to the variable interest entity.

Therefore, a legal entity is identified as a variable interest entity if any of these conditions are met.

The equity investment at risk is not sufficient to finance its activities without additional subordinated financial support or, as a group, the holders of the equity investment at risk lack any one of the following three characteristics:

- the power, through voting rights or similar rights, to direct the activities of an entity that most significantly impact the entity's economic performance;
- the obligation to absorb the expected losses of the entity;
- the right to receive the expected residual returns of the entity.

Interesting to note, it clarifies that in order to direct the activities of a variable interest entity, the enterprise does not have to exercise it (FASB 167, 2009:para. 14B).

Under the FASB Accounting Standards Update No. 2015-02 (February 2015) two primary models were identified for determining if an entity has to be consolidated, specifically the *voting interest entity model* and the *VIE model*. The former relies on the general rule prescribed by ARB 51 for legal entities other than limited partnership, whilst the latter relies on prescriptions advanced by SFAS 167. With reference to variable interest entities, no substantial changes have been made with reference to the issue here at stake.

2.3.2 Reporting boundaries and minority interests

The topic of boundaries cannot be appropriately addressed without also taking into consideration minority interests. The inclusion or exclusion of this category of interests (currently known as non-controlling interests) within the reporting boundaries of an organisation brings technical and conceptual implications that are crucial for understanding what an entity is (see Chapter 4), and how value, in this case equity, is determined. It is therefore not surprising that this theme has been subject to a longstanding debate internationally and nationally within the financial accounting literature (Lopes et al., 2013; Pizzo, 1989; So and Smith, 2009), and especially among the accounting standard setters, such as IASB (formerly IASC) and FASB. Although the accounting treatment of non-controlling interests today is clearly regulated by standards, this has not always been the case. As pointed out by Clark (1993) a consensus towards the definition and nature of minority interests has been only recently been agreed. Since their first appearance at the beginning of the 1900s, they have been referred to variously as liability, equity or even neither of the two and hence their displacement has also varied. Furthermore, in the rare cases when they were defined, nothing was stated about their nature. It was during the 1940s that scholars started to take positions about the nature of these interests. Despite recognising them as 'outside interests', the American Accounting Association (AAA) remained silent about the theoretical apparatus that informed its choices (Kohler and Scovill, 1938 and AAA, 1955). On the contrary, it was the proponents of the alternative view, which conceived them as equity, who made a major step towards the conceptual contribution which illustrated the choice to define minority interests as liability or equity. The initial key proponent in this respect was Moonitz in extending the entity theory elaborated by Paton. As he stated "minority interest serves as a reminder that complete community of interest in the affiliated companies does not exist, and the divergence of interest must be recognized" (Moonitz, 1942, p. 241). Since then, different orientations have been espoused in order to recognise minority interests. For example, International Accounting Standard no. 3 issued by the Accountants International Study Group in 1972 advanced the 'parent company view' and minority interests were to be shown as a separate item. In Europe, the EC 7th Directive and the transposition of IAS 27 into Italian jurisdiction, embodied by Legislative Decree No. 127/1991, have somehow identified interim steps towards a recognition of minority interests within the reporting boundaries. IAS 3 indirectly advanced the view that they should be included within the equity, while the latter represented a more contradictory situation. According to Legislative Decree no. 127/1991 minority interests have to be compulsorily included in the consolidated equity, whilst no clear indication is provided as to where to insert them in the income statement.

Only recently an official position towards the identification of minority interests within the equity occurred, with the revisions of IAS 27 (2008) and IFRS 3 (2008). Under IAS 27, "minority interests should be presented in the consolidated balance sheet within equity, but separate from the parent's shareholders' equity. Minority interests in the profit or loss of the group should also be separately disclosed" [IAS 27:33]. Furthermore, for each transaction undertaken, an entity may choose between two different measurement method options – fair value or the proportionate share of the acquiree's identifiable net assets [IFRS 3(2008):19]. If fair value is chosen, its subsequent changes are not recognised [IAS 27(2008):18(c)]. The total comprehensive income has to be attributed to the owners of the parent and to the non-controlling interests, even if this results in the non-controlling interests having a deficit balance [IAS 27(2008):28]. This view has also been confirmed by IFRS 10, which superseded IAS 27 in 2011.

The perspective espoused by IASB to leave entities free to adopt one measurement method or another can be seen as deriving from a more conceptual alignment to the 'entity view'.

At the same time in the US, accounting for minority interests was considerably modified and regulated when FASB released two new standards in 2007 related to business combinations, namely Statement no. 160, which amended ARB no. 51, and Statement no. 141(R).

As stated by the FASB itself, this decision relied on the acknowledgement that until then the variety of practices which existed in the accounting treatment and reporting of minority interests were at the expense of comparability (between practices and with IFRS) and clarity:

> Before this Statement was issued, limited guidance existed for reporting non-controlling interests. As a result, considerable diversity in practice existed. [. . .] This Statement, together with the IASB's Amendments to IAS 27, *Consolidated and Separate Financial Statements*, concludes a

joint effort by the Board and IASB to improve the accounting for and reporting of noncontrolling interests in consolidated financial statements while promoting the international convergence of accounting standards.

(FASB Statement no. 160, 2007:ii;iv)

As pointed out by Bahnson et al. (2008), the development of these standards has signified "more than a name change" (from 'minority' to 'non-controlling'). There are two main areas of change that are of interest for the issue here under discussion. The first modification concerns the displacement of non-controlling interests (NCI) in the consolidated financial statements. Within the balance sheet, NCI must be located within the equity section of the consolidated balance sheet as a separate line item and no longer in the mezzanine section, as had been common practice until 2007. As for consolidated income statements and comprehensive income, the standard can likewise be seen as requiring a major level of transparency. Consolidated income statements must present the net income for the whole enterprise, as well as the allocations to the parent and the NCI. The same will be the case for accumulated other comprehensive income. With reference to the cash flow statement and statement of changes in equity, the outcome of the events of the period will be presented for the whole consolidated enterprise, and the eventual modifications between the initial and final NCI balances will be included in an additional column in the equity statement. From these changes advanced by Statement no. 160 (introduced by Statement no. 141(R)), another two changes emerge. The reporting entity is now conceived as the entire economic enterprise created as result of the combination and NCI will be considered as stockholders' equity.

In terms of measurement, both standards provide increased indications. Statement no. 141 (R) requires the assets and liabilities of a subsidiary to be recorded at fair value as of the acquisition date (thus rendering them comparable with those of the parent's portions). In the case of partially owned subsidiaries, Statement no. 160 requires the NCI's proportional claim to the difference between the fair values of the subsidiary's assets and liabilities to be reported within consolidated equity. Analogous to the revisions made to IAS 27 and IFRS 3, these amendments have been acknowledged as mirroring the adoption of the different theories that underlie consolidation and, in this particular case, of the entity theory. As stated by Bahnson et al. (2008):

> These modifications reflect an application of the entity accounting theory that will cause financial statements to reflect all shareholder interests, including those of the parent and subsidiary's noncontrolling shareholders. Existing accounting for the NCI is a slapdash mix of

practices that is not aligned with any particular concept and certainly does not produce information useful for rational decisions. This explicit adoption of the entity theory also is consistent with FASB's Concepts Statement no. 6 classification of the NCI as a residual equity interest. (www.journalofaccountancy.com/issues/2008/nov/noncontrollinginterestmuchmorethananamechange.html)

2.4 Conclusion

The aim of this Chapter has been to review the main theories and pronouncements that underlie the regulation of company and group financial reporting. In particular, the views put forth by the key standard setters, namely the International Accounting Standards Board (IASB) and the Financial Accounting Standards Board (FASB) on consolidation and on the principal technical and measurement implications that derive from them, such as the treatment of special purpose entities and of non-controlling (minority) interests, have been presented. From the analysis conducted it appears clear that the logics that underpin the development of accounting standards and pronouncements in relation to consolidation have been quite varied. The same can be maintained with reference to the treatment of special purpose entities and minority interests. In particular, as to the latter, it is possible to state that although it took almost 50 years to clearly recognise non-controlling interest, both the IASB and FASB have somehow reached a consensus both in terms of technical (displacement) and measurement aspects, as well as of theories that underpin approaches, which can be seen as been mainly embodied by the entity view.

Notes

1 Often, 'entity' and 'proprietary' are conceived as representing alternative views of the so-called "orientation postulate" (Zeff, 1978). For instance, Baxter (1984) treats them as a sort of 'pre-accounting ideas': "[T]he shareholders' viewpoint [i.e. the proprietary theory] seems the more human and democratic. My own inclination is to say that it should win" (Baxter, 1984:27). Though recognising these views, the terms 'entity' and 'proprietary' will be used for referring to the theories and conceptualisations underlying them.
2 "A Member State shall require any undertaking governed by its national law to draw up consolidated accounts and a consolidated annual report if that undertaking (a parent undertaking):

   (a) has a majority of the shareholders' or members' voting rights in another undertaking (a subsidiary undertaking); or
   (b) has the right to appoint or remove a majority of the members of the administrative, management or supervisory body of another undertaking (a subsidiary undertaking) and is at the same time a shareholder in or member of that undertaking; or

(c) has the right to exercise a dominant influence over an undertaking (a subsidiary undertaking) of which it is a shareholder or member, pursuant to a contract entered into with that undertaking or to a provision in its memorandum or articles of association, where the law governing that subsidiary undertaking permits its being subject to such contracts or provisions. A Member State need not prescribe that a parent undertaking must be a shareholder in or member of its subsidiary undertaking.

[. . .]

"Article 33

1. Where an undertaking included in a consolidation exercises a significant influence over the operating and financial policy of an undertaking not included in the consolidation (an associated undertaking) in which it holds a participating interest, as defined in Article 17 of Directive 78/660/EEC, that participating interest shall be shown in the consolidated balance sheet as a separate item with an appropriate heading. An undertaking shall be presumed to exercise a significant influence over another undertaking where it has 20% or more of the shareholders' or members' voting rights in that undertaking."

3 Even though IFRS 12 regards only disclosures, we consider it as a part of a wider and unitary set of standards for defining and informing on boundaries within consolidated accounts.

Bibliography

Accountants International Study Group (1972), *International accounting standard no. 3*.

Accounting Principles Board (1970), *Accounting Principles Board (APB) opinionno. 16 business combinations*. (http://www.fasb.org/cs/BlobServer?blobkey=id&blobnocache=true&blobwhere=1175820194221&blobheader=application%2Fpdf&blobheadername2=Content-Length&blobheadername1=Content-Disposition&blobheadervalue2=118985&blobheadervalue1=filename%3Dapb16.pdf&blobcol=urldata&blobtable=MungoBlobs)

Alexander, D. (2015), Directive 2013/34/EU, article 6 an analysis and some implications. A research note, *Financial Reporting*, 1, pp. 5–22.

American Accounting Association (1955), Committee on concepts and standards, consolidated financial statements, supplementary statement No. 7, *The Accounting Review*, pp. 194–197.

Anthony, R. N. (1975), *Accounting for the cost of interest* (Lexington, MA: Lexington Books-D. C. Heath and Co).

Ardemani, E. (1968), L'evoluzione del concetto di impresa e dei sistemi contabili in Italia [The evolution of firm concept and accounting systems in Italy], *Rivista dei dottori commercialisti*, 3(May–June), pp. 411–430.

Bahnson, P. R., MCallister, B. P., and Miller, P. B. W. (2008), Noncontrolling interest: Much more than a name change, *Journal of Accountancy*. (https://www.journalofaccountancy.com/issues/2008/nov/noncontrollinginterestmuchmorethananamechange.html)

Baxter, W. (1984), *Inflation accounting* (Oxford: Philip Allan).

Clark, M. W. (1993). Evolution of concepts of minority interest. *Accounting Historians Journal*, 20(1), pp. 59–78.

Committee on Accounting Procedure of the AICPA (1959), *Accounting Research Bulletin (ARB) 51 Consolidated Financial Statements*.

EEC no. 349/83 on *Consolidated Accounts*.

EU Directive no. 34/2013 on *The annual financial statements, consolidated financial statements and related reports of certain types of undertakings*.

Financial Accounting Standards Board (FASB) (1987), *Statement of financial accounting standards no. 94*. (http://www.fasb.org/summary/stsum94.shtml)

Financial Accounting Standards Board (FASB) (2001), *Statement of financial accounting standards no. 141*. (http://www.xavierpaper.com/documents/usgaap/n.Fas141.pdf)

Financial Accounting Standards Board (FASB) (2003), *Interpretation (FIN) no. 46*. (http://www.fasb.org/summary/finsum46r.shtml)

Financial Accounting Standards Board (FASB) (2007, Revised), *Statement of financial accounting standards no. 141*. (http://www.fasb.org/jsp/FASB/Document_C/DocumentPage?cid=1218220124931&acceptedDisclaimer=true)

Financial Accounting Standards Board (FASB) (2007), *Statement of financial accounting standards no. 160*. (http://www.fasb.org/jsp/FASB/Document_C/DocumentPage?cid=1218220125561&acceptedDisclaimer=true)

Financial Accounting Standards Board (FASB) (2009), *Statement of financial accounting standards no. 167*. (https://asc.fasb.org/cs/BlobServer?blobkey=id&blobnocache=true&blobwhere=1175820928961&blobheader=application%2Fpdf&blobheadername2=Content-Length&blobheadername1=Content-Disposition&blobheadervalue2=577963&blobheadervalue1=filename%3Dfas167.pdf&blobcol=urldata&blobtable=MungoBlobs)

Financial Accounting Standards Board (FASB) (2015), *Accounting standards update no. 2015–02*. (https://asc.fasb.org/imageRoot/92/63493892.pdf)

Hatfield, H. R. (1909), *Modern accounting* (New York: D. Appleton & Co).

International Accounting Standards Board (IASB) (2004), *IFRS 3 business combinations* (Author: London).

International Accounting Standards Board (IASB) (2008), *IAS 27 Consolidated and separate financial statements* (IASB: London).

International Accounting Standards Board (IASB) (2008), *IFRS 3 Business combinations* (IASB: London).

International Accounting Standards Board (IASB) (2011), *IAS 27 Consolidated and separate financial statements* (IASB: London).

International Accounting Standards Board (IASB) (2011), *IAS 28 investments in associates and joint ventures, international financial reporting standards* (IASB: London).

International Accounting Standards Board (IASB) (2011), *IFRS 11 Joint arrangements, international financial reporting standards* (IASB: London).

International Accounting Standards Board (IASB) (2011), *IFRS 12 disclosure of interests in other entities, international financial reporting standards* (IASB: London).

International Accounting Standards Board (IASB) (2013), *IFRS 10 consolidated financial statements, international financial reporting standards* (IASB: London).

International Accounting Standards Committee (IASC) (1983), *IAS 22 business combinations* (IASB: London).

Kell, W. G. (1953), Should the accounting entity be personified? *The Accounting Review*, 28(1), pp. 40–43.

Kester, R. B. (1917–1918), *Accounting theory and practice*, 2 Vols (New York: Ronald Press).

Kohler, E. L., and Scovill, H. T. (1938), Some tentative propositions underlying consolidated reports, *The Accounting Review*, 13(1), pp. 63–77.

Li, D. H. (1960a, April), The nature of corporate residual equity under the entity concept, *The Accounting Review*, 35, pp. 258–263.

Li, D. H. (1960b, October), The nature and treatment of dividends under the entity concept, *The Accounting Review*, 35, pp. 674–679.

Lopes, A. I., Lourenço, I., and Soliman, M. (2013), Do alternative methods of reporting non-controlling interests really matter? *Australian Journal of Management*, 38(1), pp. 7–30.

Moonitz, M. (1942), The entity approach to consolidated statements, *The Accounting Review*, 17(3), pp. 236–242.

Moonitz, M. (1951), *The entity theory of consolidated statements* (Brooklyn: Foundation Press).

Paton, W. A. (1922), *Accounting theory* (New York: Ronald Press).

Pizzo, M. (1989), Minority interests and the Italian experience, *Economia Aziendale*, 8(3), pp. 323–338.

SIC-12 (1998), *Consolidation – Special purpose entities*.

So, S., and Smith, M. (2009), Value relevance of IAS 27 (2003), revision on presentation of non-controlling interest: Evidence from Hong Kong, *Journal of International Financial Management & Accounting*, 20(2), pp. 166–198.

Sprague, Ch. E. (1907), *The philosophy of accounts* (New York: Published by the author).

Staubus, G. J. (1959), The residual equity point of view in accounting, *The Accounting Review*, 34(1), pp. 3–13.

Suojanen, W. W. (1954), Accounting theory and the large corporation, *The Accounting Review*, 29(3), pp. 391–398.

Zeff, S. A. (1978), *A critical examination of the orientation postulate in accounting* (New York: Arno Press – orig. ed., 1961, University of Michigan).

3 Boundaries in non-financial reporting

Within the non-financial reporting arena, the emergence of new forms of reporting practices, such as sustainability, intellectual capital (or intangibles) and the advent of integrated reporting has lead the related organisations operating in this field to develop guidelines, frameworks and standards to support the reporting of these type of information. In addition to setting principles and content elements that inform the reporting processes, these documents also tackle the problem associated with the identification and definition of reporting boundaries. In this Chapter, the discussion focusses on the principal changes that have occurred in the identification and definition of reporting boundaries compared to the most recent versions of these frameworks and guidelines.

Within the *sustainability arena*, the following are examined:

- the Guidelines and Standards issued by the Global Reporting Initiative (GRI),
- the Framework developed by the Climate Disclosure Standards Board (CDSB),
- the Greenhouse Gas (GHG) Protocol,
- the Framework and Standards released by the Sustainability Accounting Standards Board (SASB),
- the Accounting for Sustainability (A4S) Guidelines on Social and Human Capital Accounting, and
- the newly released Recommendations by the Task Force on Climate-related Financial Disclosure set up by the Financial Stability Board in 2017.

With reference to the value-based approaches:

- the World Intellectual Capital Initiative (WICI) Intangibles Reporting Framework, and
- the International <IR> Framework released by the International Integrated Reporting Council (IIRC).

In addition to these standards and frameworks, *ad hoc* projects that resulted in documents being issued by GRI (GRI Boundary Protocol) and CDSB (Proposals for boundary setting in mainstream reports) on the problem of reporting boundaries will also be analysed and, finally, the requirements advanced by the Directive on Non-Financial Information (2014/95/EU) issued by the European Commission in 2014 will be illustrated.

3.1 The sustainability reporting approaches

3.1.1 The GRI Guidelines, the GRI Boundary Protocol and the GRI Standards

> The **Global Reporting Initiative (GRI)** is an independent international organisation that has pioneered sustainability reporting since 1997. Its origins lie in the effort of US non-profit organisations the Coalition for Environmentally Responsible Economies (CERES) and the Tellus Institute, with the involvement of the United Nations Environment Programme (UNEP) (www.globalreporting.org/information/about-gri/gri-history/Pages/GRI's%20history.aspx).

With reference to defining and identifying boundaries, GRI can be seen as the longest existing organisation compared to the others. The initial steps towards the elaboration of this aspect were undertaken only a few years after its establishment in 1997. In 2002, the second edition of the Guidelines was released, which already contained some indications about boundaries. Even though no operational processes were suggested, the underlying logic was clear: companies should base their boundary setting mechanisms on the interaction with stakeholders and on the principle of transparency. This way they would be better able to "reflect the unique 'footprint' of their organisation and their activities" (GRI Guidelines, 2002:15). In this edition of the Guidelines, the theme of boundaries was included under the reporting principle of 'completeness', which was considered as three-dimensional, incorporating the 'operational boundary dimension', the 'scope dimension' and the 'temporal dimension'. It is interesting to note that, in contrast to financial reporting, the term 'boundary' was conceived as being different from 'scope'. The document states that, "boundary [relates to] the range of entities for which the reporting organisation gathers data". It is identified on the basis of the economic, social and environmental impacts of an organisation and its definition can be related to various elements, such as financial control, legal ownership etc. Boundaries vary depending on the nature of the information reported. Scope, meanwhile, is strictly linked to those aspects for which the Guidelines present indicators and queries. Hence, in the view of GRI, these two notions can and cannot be equalised. Boundaries take into consideration the impacts that correspond to the scope, or can be broader or narrower. In view of this, it is recommended that efforts should be made to match the scope with the boundary and, if this is not the case, differences should be explained (Sustainability Reporting Guidelines, 2002:34).

Following the release of the 2002 Guidelines, GRI undertook an *ad hoc* project from October 2002 to December 2004 called the 'GRI Boundary Protocol Project'. The aim of this project has been to provide guidance to organisations that were using the GRI guidelines, "including definitions of boundaries and procedures for setting reporting boundaries" (GRI Project Fact Sheet, 2003:1). Indeed, the Initiative recognised that in similar fashion to financial reporting, sustainability reporting also needs clear guidance on how to set boundaries. In addition, according to GRI, a centralised and unitary project on this topic would have led to an increase in the consistency and comparability of those reports that adopted the GRI Guidelines (GRI Project Fact Sheet, 2003). As maintained by the Leader of the Working Group on the GRI Boundary Protocol:

> We started the boundaries work to respond to need expressed by numerous stakeholders (including business) for recognizing that many critical sustainability impacts happen outside of immediate operations and that GRI needed to provide guidance on how to reflect these issues in reporting. At the same time, there was also a need to consider how to address the question of sustainability context and impacts associated with a company.
>
> (Sean Gilbert, Leader of the Working Group on the GRI Boundary Protocol)

The project was articulated in four main phases:

- the preparation of background materials by the GRI Secretariat,
- convening the extant models on reporting boundaries in sustainability performance measurement and financial accounting,
- drafting the protocol through face-to-face meetings by a multi-stakeholders Boundaries Working Group (BWG), and a public comment period, and finally
- the submission of the final draft to the GRI Governing Body.

Boundaries in non-financial reporting 47

It is interesting that despite the sustainability focus of the Initiative and of the project, financial reporting is included as a topic and as an area of expertise in both the background materials and the individuals to be involved in the BWG, perhaps implying the central importance of financial reporting.

As a result of this project, the Protocol was released in January 2005. As previously mentioned, financial reporting and especially the standards advanced to govern its recognition, measurement and reporting, namely IFRS, have been recognised as a fundamental reference point for the definition of reporting boundaries. Indeed, it states that "financial control is a common boundary for disclosure" (GRI Boundary Protocol, 2005:2). In addition, from a conceptual and procedural perspective, financial reporting principles have been identified as a baseline, even if they are not the only one:

> *This protocol has aligned its concept of control/influence with financial reporting principles as the baseline, but has expanded the definition of significant influence to take into account certain non-financial sources of significant influence.* It recognises that there are different types of disclosures in a sustainability report including indicators focused on operations, indicators related to management approaches, and more general narrative disclosures on strategies adopted or dilemmas recognized (figure 2.1). Boundary setting under this protocol is structured to recognise the differences between these types of disclosure.
> (GRI Boundary Protocol, 2005:5, emphasis added)

> The four rules listed below should govern decisions on setting a boundary and their disclosure. These principles are derived from and are compatible with the reporting principles in Part B of the Guidelines, particularly completeness, comparability, relevance, inclusiveness, and sustainability context. *They have also been developed with financial reporting principles in mind.*
> (GRI Boundary Protocol, 2005:6, emphasis added)

A result of this rationale is that the definition of the reporting boundary derives from the intertwining of two concepts: 'impact' and 'control/influence'. 'Impact', and especially 'significant impacts', are defined as "those that change a performance measured under a quantitative indicator by a noticeable amount" (GRI Boundary Protocol, 2005:11). 'Control' is the "power to govern the financial and operating policies of an enterprise in order to obtain benefits from its activities" and 'significant influence' is "the power to participate in the financial and operating policy decisions of the entity but is not

48 *Boundaries in non-financial reporting*

control over those policies". If compared to the definitions provided by IAS and IFRS (see Chapter 2), it appears that both these ideas have been borrowed from international accounting standards. As pointed out by the Leader of the Working Group on the GRI Boundary Protocol:

> We wanted to have a broad alignment with systems for financial reporting, but were not specifically looking to build from accounting standards. However, as we looked at many of the challenges around defining boundaries, we found that many of the definitions and ideas in accounting were helpful for our purposes even if they led to different results in the context of financial accounting. For example, influence was a core concept for our boundary protocol and we found that the technical definition of influence shared by some of the accounting members was actually quite relevant and close to what the Working Group was seeking to express.
>
> (Sean Gilbert, Leader of the Working Group on the GRI Boundary Protocol)

The GRI G3 Guidelines (2006) have been informed by this Protocol. According to the Guidelines, the boundary setting process relates to the specific concepts of 'control' and of 'significant influence', combined with the nature of the performance (indicator) to be disclosed (which can be operational, management or narrative). The decision to combine the two stems from the acknowledgement that the different nature of the relationships with other entities determines differing levels of information accessibility and of possible ways to affect the outcomes for an organisation. Therefore, according to GRI, the entities which should be included in a sustainability report are those that: "generate significant sustainability impacts (actual and potential) and/or all entities over which the reporting organization exercises control or significant influence with regard to financial and operating policies and practices" (GRI G3 Guidelines, 2006:18). This is the case even if only a minimum level of disclosure is required. Indeed, the Guidelines prescribe that those entities over which control is exercised should be covered by indicators of operational performance, while in the case of significant influence the Disclosure on Management Approach should be used. If entities that generate significant impacts and are not under the control of significant influence are at stake, they should be included in the boundaries of narrative disclosures. Conditions of exclusion are assumed in the name of efficiency, and if this does not substantially affect the final result of a disclosure or indicator. Interestingly, the definition of entity is quite different from that used in financial reporting. The Guidelines define it rather vaguely, but link it strictly to the notion of boundary. It is maintained that an entity is: "An organization or sometimes an operation that is considered for inclusion or exclusion from a reporting boundary, no matter whether it is a legally constituted body" (GRI G3 Guidelines, 2006:13). Similarly, it should be noted that the term 'scope' continues to be conceptualised and used in a different manner from financial reporting; it is not equated to the term 'boundary' but is much broader and includes the role of stakeholders.

> Scope refers to the range of sustainability topics covered in a report. The sum of the topics and Indicators reported should be sufficient to reflect significant economic, environmental, and social impacts. It should also enable stakeholders to assess the organization's performance.
> (GRI G3 Guidelines, 2006:14)

The GRI G4 Guidelines released in 2013 developed further, and define the reporting content through four main principles: stakeholder inclusiveness, sustainability context, materiality and completeness. More specifically, the process to delineate reporting boundaries is regulated by standards disclosure G17–G23 composed of four phases: identification; prioritisation; validation; and review.

The first step to identification refers to the choice of topics considered as 'relevant'. They are those that may reasonably be considered important for reflecting the organisation's economic, environmental and social impacts; or influencing the assessments and decisions of stakeholders (G4–G18), together with the so-called GRI Aspects which are those subjects covered by the Guidelines for which GRI Indicators and disclosures on management approach (DMA) have been developed. For each relevant topic, the organisation has to identify the boundary that is related to the concept of impact (defined as the significant economic, environmental and social impacts that are: positive, negative, actual, potential, direct, indirect, short term, long term, intended, unintended) and where it occurs (within or outside the organisation or both). In the case of impacts that occur within the organisation, it is necessary to identify which entities are affected by the impact, as not all of them may be (the entities considered within the organisation are all of those included in the organisation's consolidated financial statements or equivalent documents, G4–G17). If the impact occurs outside the organisation, the relevant impact should be captured. These relevant impacts can be described as direct or indirect for some topics, or as caused by, contributed to, or linked to the organisation for others. Finally, in the case of impacts *within* and *outside* the organisation (for example in relation to emissions), the identification relates to a combination of the above considerations.

The second stage of prioritisation relies on the application of the principles of materiality and stakeholder inclusiveness. This is in order to assess each aspect considered relevant to the organisation's economic, environmental and social impacts and the influence on stakeholder assessments and decisions.

The third step refers to the assessment of the list of material aspects (defined as the range of aspects covered in a report), against the scope, boundaries and time to ensure that the report provides a reasonable and balanced representation of the organisation's significant economic, environmental and social impacts, and enables stakeholders to assess the organisation's performance.

In addition, it refers to the approval of the list of identified material aspects by the relevant internal senior decision-maker. This involves preparing systems and processes to gather the information which needs to be disclosed, translating the material aspects which have been identified into Standard Disclosures to report against (DMA and Indicators). The available information needs to be determined, items for which there is still the need to establish management approaches and measurement systems need to be explained.

The final step relates to the review of those aspects that were material in the previous reporting period which are then used to inform Step 1 of the new reporting cycle. As compared to the G3 Guidelines, it is worthy of note that the main element modified has been the criteria which are to be adopted in order to identify the entities that should be included (or excluded) in the boundary. The notions of 'control' and of 'significant influence' have been abandoned and the determinant for boundary setting is now related to the link between the impact and the material aspect. To put it another way, the boundary is (generally) set on the basis of where impacts relating to a material aspect occur. Impacts for each material aspect must be identified and described both inside and outside the organisation. If impacts on material aspects occur outside the organisation (where the definition of 'outside the organisation' has remained unmodified, and still refers to consolidated financial statements or equivalent documents), indicators are reported if quality data is available.

This approach was further streamlined in the GRI Standards released in October 2016, which come into force in July 2018, thus superseding the G4 Guidelines. As the GRI itself states:

> The concept of Boundary [...] is arguably one of the most challenging areas of sustainability reporting, and was inconsistently understood by G4 reporters. This concept has now been simplified in the GRI Standards, to be more clear and to align more closely with key international references.
>
> (GRI website, www.globalreporting.org/standards/questions-and-feedback/materiality-and-topic-boundary/)

The principal modifications to boundary setting specifically relate to the concept of 'impact' and have been inspired by the UN 'Guiding Principles on Business and Human Rights' and the OECD Guidelines for Multinational Enterprises. Indeed, to comply with the GRI Standards and, especially, with GRI 103: Management Approach (which sets out the requirements about how an organisation has to manage a material topic) a description of 'where' the impact occurs and 'how the organisation is involved with it' is required. Accordingly, information must be reported with reference to:

- the entities where impacts occur (which include entities in the consolidated financial statement or equivalent documents);
- the impacts that an organisation causes, has contributed to, and that are directly linked with its activities, products or services through a business relationship (which include relationships with business partners, entities in its value chain); and
- any other non-state or state entity directly linked to its business operations, products or services).

(GRI 103: Management Approach, 2016:6)

Interestingly, even if an organisation does not have the ability to effect change on the organisation that is causing or contributing to the impact, it is still expected to report on it and on its 'mitigating activities'. Furthermore, in the case of a boundary that extends beyond the organisation, particularly when it is not possible to access all the information the organisation needs in order to report on the impact, the illustration of the management approach undertaken is still required, even though the reasons for omission for topic-specific disclosure can be used.

3.1.2 The CDSB Discussion Paper and Framework

> **The Climate Disclosure Standards Board (CDSB)** was formed in 2007 as a consortium created by the World Economic Forum in order to respond to the concerns expressed by its members regarding the lack of comparable, comprehensive, accessible and understandable information on climate-related information for use by investors, trustees, directors and managers.
>
> It is now recognised as an international consortium of business and environmental NGOs committed to advancing and aligning the global mainstream corporate reporting model to equate natural capital with financial capital (www.cdsb.net/our-story).

Similar to GRI, the Climate Disclosure Standards Board (CDSB) in 2014 released a discussion paper aiming to synthesise the extant options for boundary setting by groups of companies for non-financial reporting purposes (GRI, IIRC, SASB, GHG Protocol). As explained by one of its authors, the aim of the discussion paper has been to: "Assist the companies for making a clear rational choice, when establishing the data boundaries for their non-financial and thus their potential integrated data. Many companies struggled (and still struggle) to find good principles for data boundaries" (Interviewee B, CEO and Lead Researcher, Centre for ESG Research, Denmark). According to the extant Guidelines, Standards and Frameworks, the main difficulties that organisations face in identifying and defining reporting boundaries/scopes relate to the vagueness of these documents, and the different backgrounds that characterise those organisational departments responsible for reporting.

> The trouble is that most guidelines usually are very vague, when it comes to data boundary definitions (and many other elements for that matter). They are thus not always useful for real corporates with internal and external leasing in and out and joint operations and other complex ownership structures like cross-ownership. Sometimes it is also a matter of that the CSR/ESG people are not aware about the financial consolidation rules – and potentially think they can add up the local statutory reports, which the local employees have provided to their authorities, potentially given operational control, and then when added up they will get a corporate report. That is obviously not possible. That is obvious if you have a financial background, and know you have to normalise the data to corporate standards and disregard operational control, to get a corporate non-financial data set that can be compared and potentially integrated with the financial dataset. But for most is this not obvious.
>
> [. . .]
>
> Another issue that has cluttered the data boundary discussion is the debate around the inclusion of up- and downstream data which is especially important in view of the recent discussions around due diligence. But it is important to understand that if we are to be able to compare two or more companies in peer-reviews, we need to be able to distinguish between what is the company's own data and what is up- & downstream data. In reality it would it be good to replicate some of the inner logic of GHG protocol's scope 1 and 3. Can you imagine having scope 3 water consumption or scope 3 human rights issues? I can. But that discussion is still missing.
>
> (Interviewee A, CEO and Lead Researcher, Centre for ESG Research, Denmark)

As a result of this exercise, six proposals have been advanced:

(1) the clarification of the link between the objectives of non-financial reporting, materiality, the audience for reporting and organisational boundary setting,
(2) the identification of a single, standardised approach to organisational boundary setting in mainstream reporting,
(3) the alignment of the consolidated group boundary with the way in which the profit and loss/comprehensive income statement is prepared (rather than with balance sheet entries).

With specific reference to the GHG Protocol which underlines the CDSB approach, it has been advanced that:

(4) within the consolidated group boundary, GHG emissions from the use of resources should be reported by the user,
(5) there should be no distinction between financial and operating leases for GHG emissions reporting purposes – the GHG emissions should be reported by the user in all cases where the use of an asset is made possible under any contractual arrangements, including a finance or operating lease, and finally that
(6) a group's policy for the preparation of consolidated climate change-related reporting should be clearly stated as part of the disclosure in the same way that financial statements include notes setting out the policies that have been applied for their preparation.

Some of these proposals have been adopted by companies as well as by some institutions. However, most of the challenges in setting reporting boundaries have remained:

> I think it has been part of the argumentation between more advanced company reporters for some years – and I can also see it has now been adopted by UNCTAD in their guidelines. My latest research shows though that most companies unfortunately still either do not inform of their data boundaries or use operational/homemade/convenient data boundaries. That is most unfortunate, as then the data cannot be integrated with the financial data in a sensible way.
> (Interviewee A, CEO and Lead Researcher, Centre for ESG Research, Denmark)

The discussion paper informed the last version of the CDSB Framework which was issued in June 2015, even though the history of the consortium has always been collaborative in nature. Since the very first elaboration of the Framework (initially titled 'Climate Change Reporting Framework' – CCRF), its ambition has been to adopt and align the relevant principles stemming from existing standards and practices (including financial reporting) and to allow them to incorporate climate change-related information. In this spirit, in October 2012 the CCRF Edition 1.0 (September 2010) was supplemented by Edition 1.1. This was in order to clarify the CDSB orientation towards the setting of organisational boundaries and, in particular, to support the practices advanced by the GHG Protocol. Accordingly, the CCRF's recommendations on organisational boundary setting can be seen as a result of an effort to compromise between the requirements set for financial reporting and the indications based on the GHG Protocol. Indeed, they are divided in two parts.

Part 1 GHG Emissions (which corresponds to Scope 1 and Scope 2 of the GHG Protocol) recommends the disclosure of those emissions deriving from the "sources and activities of entities for which consolidated financial statements are prepared" (CDSB Framework Edition 1.1, 2012:31). Part 2 relates to those aspects (emissions) that lie outside the boundaries of consolidated financial statements, namely those "from investments in associates" and any Scope 1 and 2 that derive from "operational controlled and/or other entities/activities/facilities that are not consolidated in Part 1" and other subject to specific conditions (CDSB Framework Edition 1.1, 2012, para. 4.26:24).

In the 2015 version of the Framework the concept of boundaries has been linked once more to 'organisational boundary' but it has been simplified somewhat compared to the previous version. It is generally defined as being the one used for mainstream reports:

> Where requirements for the preparation of mainstream reports, or elements of mainstream reports, prescribe the entities and activities that should be included within the boundary of the reporting organisation, the same organisational boundary should be used for reporting environmental information according to the CDSB Framework.
>
> (CDSB Framework, 2015:24)

However, in the case of environmental information which lies outside the boundaries it is stated that:

> In some cases, environmental information outside the organisation's mainstream reporting boundary may be disclosed for a variety of reasons, including:
>
> • The reporting organisation is required or chooses to report on activities for which it is responsible (whether or not within the mainstream reporting boundary),

- Due to the nature of the contract for the operation or use of or services procured from the entity or facility, the reporting organisation is exposed to material risk, opportunity or financial impact, and
- The reporting organisation has the power to influence its environmental impacts.

(CDSB Framework, 2015:24–25)

Notably, one of these refers to the power of the reporting organisation to influence its environmental impacts, which is defined as "changes in the condition of the environment. Environmental impacts can be positive or negative, direct or indirect and may manifest as short or long-term changes to the balance, stock, flow, availability and quality of natural capital" (CDSB Framework, 2015:7). From this definition, it is possible to derive two additional observations. Firstly, the term 'power' is used similarly to financial reporting even if in this case it is not clearly defined. Secondly, the term 'impacts' is used similarly to the way GRI does in G4 Guidelines.

Finally, according to the CDSB Framework, if there is reported information which falls outside the organisational boundary set for mainstream reporting, these should be distinguished from those related to entities that fall within the boundary, while for information which is excluded from the financial reporting boundaries, explanations should be provided.

3.1.3 The GHG Protocol, the SASB Standards, the A4S Guidelines and the TFCD Recommendations

In addition to the above standards and frameworks, the approaches proposed by GHG Protocol, SASB, A4S and the Task Force on Climate-related Financial Disclosures established by the Financial Stability Board are also pertinent.

The **Greenhouse Gas Protocol (GHG Protocol)** does not derive from the effort of a single organisation but reflects the results of the collaboration between a multi-stakeholder group involving representatives of preparers and report users. It is supported by organisations such as the World Business Council for Sustainable Development (WBCSD) and the World Resources Institute (WRI) which in the late 1990s recognised the need for an international standard for corporate GHG accounting and reporting. It currently provides standards, guidance, tools and training for business and government to measure and manage climate-warming emissions (www.ghgprotocol.org/about-us).

The theme of boundaries has been addressed by GHG since its initial development. Compared to the other approaches discussed in the previous sections, the approach to identifying and defining reporting boundaries set out in the GHG document appears much more articulated in the author's view. The first document issued by the GHG Protocol in 2001, the *Greenhouse Gas Protocol – A corporate accounting and reporting standard*, included detailed guidance about how to define both organisational and operational boundaries which were consistent with financial reporting. It states: "Where possible, it makes sense to follow company-specific distinctions [between 'control' and 'significant influence'] already in place for financial accounting, provided these are explicitly explained and followed consistently" (Greenhouse Gas Protocol, 2001:15). In particular, in order to set organisational boundaries, two concepts are adopted, specifically 'control' and 'significant influence'. Control is defined as "the ability of a company to direct the operating policies of another entity/facility", while significant influence is determined based on the following factors: "the company owns voting interests of between 20 and 50 percent; the company has the power to participate in the entity's/facility's financial and operating policy decisions and the company has a long-term interest in the entity/facility" (Greenhouse Gas Protocol, 2001:15). In terms of reporting, this distinction implies the use of two methods. In the case of both wholly owned, and not wholly owned but controlled entities/facilities, emissions are reported in total (100%). In the other cases (jointly controlled and when a significant influence exists), the equity share method is used, which accounts for the percentage of economic interest in/benefit derived from an operation. After having determined which are the entities that an organisation owns or controls, operational boundaries must be set. In relation to operational boundaries, the concepts of direct and indirect emissions emerge. Direct emissions are those deriving from sources that are owned or controlled by the company, while indirect emissions are conceived as a consequence of the activity of the company but which occur at sources owned or controlled. Another concept that supports the definition of direct and indirect emissions is the one of scope. The Protocol identifies three distinct scopes as follows:

- direct GHG emissions that are those deriving from sources that are owned or controlled by the reporting entity (Scope 1),
- GHG emissions from imports of electricity, steam or heat (Scope 2), and
- other indirect GHG emissions that are a consequence of the activities of the reporting company, but occur from sources owned or controlled by another company (Scope 3).

The revised version of the Protocol released in 2004 largely confirms this approach. Indeed, it requires reporting entities to determine organisational boundaries, operational boundaries and the scope of accounting and reporting. In order to define organisational boundaries, GHG emissions data can be consolidated according to the equity share and the control approaches. Under the equity share approach, the share of equity in the operation embodies the determinant for accounting for GHG emissions from operations. The perspective of the 2004 Protocol is that the equity share reflects economic interest conceived as "the extent of rights a company has to the risks and rewards flowing from an organisation" (GHG Protocol, 2004:17). In the case of equity share that is not aligned with the company's percentage ownership, the economic substance overrides the legal ownership, as consistent with the international financial reporting standards. Under the control approach, the company accounts on the basis of control, which is distinguished in the 2004 version as being either financial or operational. Financial control is defined as "the ability to direct the financial and operating policies with a view of gaining economic benefits from its activities" (GHG Protocol, 2004:17), while operational control is defined as "full authority of a company to introduce and implement its operating policies at the operation" (GHG Protocol, 2004:17). For operational boundaries, the same process as that outlined in the Protocol of 2001 is used, even though a link is created between the distinction of direct and indirect emissions and the consolidation method used to set organisational boundaries. Once selected, the operational boundary is then applied at each operational level. Therefore, all boundaries, operational, organisational, and of scope are respectively defined as: "GHG accounting and reporting boundaries can have several dimensions, i.e. organizational, operational, geographic, business unit, and target boundaries. The inventory boundary determines which emissions are accounted and reported by the company" (GHG Protocol, 2004:96).

> The boundaries that determine the direct and indirect emissions associated with operations owned or controlled by the reporting company. This assessment allows a company to establish which operations and sources cause direct and indirect emissions, and to decide which indirect emissions to include that are a consequence of its operations.
> [...]
> The boundaries that determine the operations owned or controlled by the reporting company, depending on the consolidation approach taken (equity or control approach).
> [...]
> The operational boundaries in relation to indirect and direct GHG emissions.
>
> (GHG Protocol, 2004:100)

> The **Sustainability Accounting Standards Board (SASB)** is an independent private-sector standards setting organisation established in 2011, dedicated to enhancing the efficiency of the capital markets by fostering high-quality disclosure of material sustainability information that meets investor needs.
>
> The SASB develops and maintains sustainability accounting standards (for 79 industries in 11 sectors) with the aim of assisting public corporations to disclose financially material information to investors in a cost-effective and decision-useful format. The SASB's transparent, inclusive, and rigorous standards-setting process is materiality focused, evidence-based and market informed (www.sasb.org/).

Regarding the SASB, the Framework released in February 2017 does not explicitly state in any detail how the reporting boundaries should be set. Specifications are provided in the industry standards that have been issued since 2011, which outlined that the approach undertaken did not differ from the ones suggested by GRI and CSDB either in nature or motivations. Indeed, the focal point in terms of 'scope of disclosure' is represented by the entities consolidated for financial reporting purposes as defined by the US GAAP and in particular for the whole entity regardless of the size of minority interests. The reason for this relates to the intention to be consistent with the other information requested for SEC filings. In the case of unconsolidated entities, the determinant for disclosure is embodied by the extent of 'necessity', i.e. the requirements of investors to understand the organisational performance in respect to sustainability issues (recognised as being typically limited to risks and opportunities associated with these entities). In terms of defining value, in contrast to the frameworks and standards presented so far, which refer to the notion of 'impact' (but not to the one of value), the SASB framework provides a definition, It specifically delineates value as "confirmatory and predictive value, which can be used to evaluate past performance and be used for future planning and decision support" (SASB Framework, 2017:4).

> The **Prince's Accounting for Sustainability Project** (A4S) was established by HRH The Prince of Wales in 2004 "to help ensure that we are not battling to meet 21st century challenges with, at best, 20th century decision making and reporting systems". Its principal aim is to inspire action by finance leaders to drive a fundamental shift towards resilient business models and a sustainable economy. In order to do this, it intends to inspire finance leaders to adopt sustainable and resilient business models, transform financial decision making to enable an integrated approach,

> reflective of the opportunities and risks posed by environmental and social issues and scale up action across the global finance and accounting community (www.accountingforsustainability.org/en/about-us/overview.html).

In June 2017, Accounting for Sustainability (A4S) also addressed the topic of reporting boundaries in its *Essential Guide to Social and Human Capital Accounting*. Although it does not refer to the whole reporting system, but only to social and human capital, it is interesting that amongst the stages identified to measure and evaluate these capitals, the first one is related to the definition of scope, defined as "the focus on the most important areas, and the relevant parts of the value chain" (A4S Essential Guide to Social and Human Capital Accounting, 2017:15). Within it, the so-called 'boundaries assessment', is determined by reference to the following:

- the identification of the type of organisational decision being made (corporate, project, product),
- the determination of where the majority and the most relevant impacts and dependencies related to risks and opportunities occur in the value chain (upstream, direct operations, downstream), and finally
- the appropriate time period to be used (historical, snapshot, financial year and expected project/product lifespan).

(A4S Essential Guide to Social and Human Capital Accounting, 2017:18)

Also in June 2017, the Task Force on Climate-related Financial Disclosures released its Recommendations Report.

> The **Task Force on Climate-related Financial Disclosures** (TFCD) was established in 2015 by the Financial Stability Board with the aim to develop voluntary, consistent climate-related financial risk disclosures for use by companies in providing information to investors, lenders, insurers, and other stakeholders.
>
> It is an industry-led task force whose general intention is to help companies understand what financial markets want from disclosure in order to measure and respond to climate change risks, and encourage firms to align their disclosures with investors' needs (www.fsb-tcfd.org/about/).

Although there is no direct and explicit reference to the theme of boundary, one of the four thematic areas around which the document is built, *Metrics and Targets*, recommends disclosure for greenhouse gas (GHG) emissions and associated metrics for historical periods in accordance with Scope 1, 2 and, if appropriate, 3[1] of the GHG Protocol and the related risks.[2] The reasons for this are associated with the acknowledgement that emissions are central to the rise of global temperature and, hence, to the increase of climate change:

> Emissions are a prime driver of rising global temperatures and, as such, are a key focal point of policy, regulatory, market, and technology responses to limit climate change. As a result, organizations with significant emissions are likely to be impacted more significantly by transition risk than other organizations. In addition, current or future constraints on emissions, either directly by emission restrictions or indirectly through carbon budgets, may impact organizations financially.
>
> (Recommendations of the Task Force on Climate-related Financial Disclosures, 2017:22)

The GHG Protocol is then identified as the main reference point: "While challenges remain, the GHG Protocol methodology is the most widely recognized and used international standard for calculating GHG emissions. Organizations may use national reporting methodologies if they are consistent with the GHG Protocol methodology" (Recommendations of the Task Force on Climate-related Financial Disclosures, 2017:22).

3.2 The 'value creation'-based approaches

3.2.1 The WICI Intangibles Framework

> The **World Intellectual Capital/Assets Initiative (WICI)** is an international collaborative network formed in 2007 which aims to promote better corporate reporting by recognising the role of intangibles/intellectual capital in the sustainability of an organisation's value generation. It acknowledges that a form of reporting able to integrate the communication of narrative and quantified information on how organisations create value through the creation, management, combination and utilisation of intangibles over the short, medium and long term is needed in the actual corporate reporting landscape.
>
> Its participants include representatives from companies, analysts and investors, the accounting profession and academia (www.wici-global.com).

With reference to the intellectual capital (IC) and intangibles field, the only documents that appear to be worthy of note to date are the *Intellectual Capital Statement – Made in Germany Guideline* (2004) published by the German Federal Ministry of Economics and Labour and the *Intangibles Reporting Framework* published by the World Intellectual Capital Initiative (WICI) in September 2016. Although the Guideline represents a national effort to support organisations in the development of an Intellectual Capital Statement (while the other is international in nature), it is interesting to note that the Guideline includes indications about how to define what it is referred to as 'System boundaries':

> In particular when an intellectual capital statement is drafted for the first time, the part of the organisation on which the work concentrates should be considered. There are almost always possibilities to define boundaries, be it locations, functions, markets or indeed individual processes. For reasons of the availability of employees, or because of risk considerations, it may make sense to start with a prototype and then in the second phase to transfer what has been learned to the rest of the organisation. Whatever the decision taken, it should be carefully documented, and it should be clearly stated in order to avoid misunderstandings as the process continues.
>
> (pp. 16–17)

The reasons why the term 'system boundaries' has been selected appear to rely on the willingness to provide a 'process view' perspective which could be distinguished from a purely legal one. As stated by one of the authors of the Guideline:

> In theory our approach is following a process oriented point of view, which means, that the systems boundaries ideally are defined according processes, not legal issues. A Process can easy over-span a legal organization (network organization) or just be a part of it.
>
> In that regard we define a system as a set of coordinated actions (processes) including all the necessary 'elements' to perform the actions. The systems boarder is where the process begins and where it ends.
>
> Some advantages of this approach are:
>
> 1. it always focusses on value adding activities of a system and therefore relevant areas of interest.
> 2. it is very flexible because it is possible to zoom in or out of processes and shift focus to relevant areas of action and performance. This is especially important if organizational boundaries are not clear like e.g. in network organizations. It is also important when

you need to manage IC based on the information generated, because management is (or should be) based on relevant information.
3. The focus is clear not abstract, and relate to daily work. e.g. if we ask about necessary assets for a process, it is clear that we mean the assets for the specific process and the responsible tasks.

But beside all the theory . . . The system boundaries in practice mostly correspond with organizational boundaries or organizational parts (e.g. business areas, divisions, processes or teams etc.).

With this definition we originally wanted to lower entrance barriers. The message was: "You do not have to start with the whole organization. You can start small and – step by step – roll out your IC management and reporting, when you know how it works and what the consequences are."

(Kay Alwert, Owner and general manager,
Alwert GmbH & Co. KG and 'core member'
of the Arbeitskreis Wissensbilanz)

Despite the step-by-step approach and the different definition of boundaries suggested by the Guideline, their setting remains a challenge also with reference to the preparation of the Intellectual Capital Statement. In one of the author's view:

Especially in network organizations or corporate groups it can be challenging to draw system boundaries. Corporate groups often have independent or semi-independent business areas. To generate the relevant information for managing these units, it is advisable to generate their own IC reports for them. But processes (and assets) in corporate groups often overlap and it is not always clear to which system they belong. A clear definition of boundaries is necessary to avoid duplication and redundancies. This is especially important when a consolidation of the results for the group's board or an external communication is needed.
[. . .]
Network organizations are another typical problem area. They often have no clear borders, because members and assets of these kind of organizations are simultaneously members or assets of other organizations as well. A typical example would be an association with voluntary personnel. Or consider an IT company with many freelance developers working with and on an open-source framework. The questions which would need to be answered when defining boundaries might be: are the freelance developers employees or suppliers? (Legally this may seem clear, but in practice it is not which may have many consequences.) Is the open-source framework an asset, a resource, a product of the

organization, or all of the above? (The answer to this question may have strong risk implications.)

(Kay Alwert, Owner and general manager, Alwert GmbH & Co. KG and 'core member' of the Arbeitskreis Wissensbilanz)

Similarly to the SASB Framework, in the WICI Framework no explicit reference is made to boundary setting, but it is possible to understand where the boundaries are cast by looking at the way 'intangibles' are conceptualised. It states that intangibles are "resources that are available for use by an organisation [...] They simply have to be available and/or utilized by the entity with the aim of generating value" (WICI Intangibles Reporting Framework, 2016:13–14). Therefore, the reporting boundary can be described best according to the concepts of assets or capital which should not be controlled but available for use. This departs from the view of traditional international financial reporting standards. As stated by the Global Chair of WICI:

The WICI Intangibles Reporting Framework (WIRF), which has been published in September 2016, does not deal explicitly with the topic of boundaries of reporting. However, while addressing the fundamental concepts of Intangibles Reporting, WIRF poses a new definition of intangibles, that is 'Intangibles are resources that are *available for use* by an organization' (WIRF, 2016:13). It is straightforward to detect that, unlike assets as defined in financial accounting (e.g., under the IASB Conceptual Framework for Financial Reporting), to include an intangible in corporate reporting an organisation does not have necessarily to own it or control it, but more simply to have access to it and use it for its own value generation processes. In this respect, WIRF states indirectly that the reporting boundaries for non-financial information on intangibles are set by the *joint conditions* of both the availability of this resource and its capacity to materially participate in the value creation of the organisation. Indeed, when reporting on intangibles follows financial reporting rules and definitions, not many of these resources appear on the face of balance sheet and in the accounts, especially if they are internally generated. In a knowledge-based and intangibles-driven economy, reporting in financial and non-financial terms has to be updated and made able to encompass a much larger classes of intangibles to better represent the value creation capacity and the value created of an organisation. This vision should inform the setting of boundaries of intangibles reporting according to WICI.

(Prof. Stefano Zambon, WICI Global Chair)

Another aspect which is analogous with the SASB Framework is the provision of a definition of value. Even though it is not directly related to the identification of reporting boundaries, WICI advances a notion of value which is articulated in "strategic value (value related to the enhancement of the competitive, market, product, reputation, and/or risk profile of the organisation) and financial value (value linked to the generation of net cash flows over time)" (WICI Intangibles Reporting Framework, 2016:13).

Therefore, it can be observed that, as compared to the 'sustainability' approaches, the 'value-creation' one based on intellectual capital and intangibles differs from the one used in financial reporting.

3.2.2 The International Integrated Reporting <IR> Framework

> Established in 2010, the **International Integrated Reporting Council (IIRC)** embodies a global coalition of regulators, investors, companies, standard setters, the accounting profession and NGOs with the aim of promoting communication about value creation as the next step in the evolution of corporate reporting. Its mission is to establish integrated reporting and thinking within mainstream business practice as the norm in the public and private sectors and its vision is to align capital allocation and corporate behaviour to wider goals of financial stability and sustainable development through the cycle of integrated reporting and thinking (https://integratedreporting.org/the-iirc-2/).

For a more holistic approach, including both a sustainability and an intangibles perspective, the case of the IIRC has to be considered. After all, the ambition for truly integrated reporting is to connect both financial and non-financial data in a value creation perspective.

The International <IR> Framework released in December 2013 by the International Integrated Reporting Council (IIRC) defines the reporting boundary of an integrated report as stemming from the combination of two aspects, which are the 'financial reporting entity' and the 'risks, opportunities and outcomes' that can be attributed or associated with the entities and stakeholders that lie beyond the financial reporting entity and that have a significant influence on the organisation's ability to create value. Indeed, it states:

> Determining the boundary for an integrated report has two aspects:
> The financial reporting entity (i.e., the boundary used for financial reporting purposes) and risks, opportunities and outcomes attributable to or associated with other entities/stakeholders beyond the financial reporting entity that have a significant effect on the ability of the financial reporting entity to create value.

> [...] The financial reporting entity identifies which subsidiaries', joint ventures' and associates' transactions and related events are included in the organization's financial report. The financial reporting entity is determined according to applicable financial reporting standards which revolve around the concepts of control or significant influence.
>
> The second aspect of determining the reporting boundary is to identify those risks, opportunities and outcomes attributable to, or associated with, entities/stakeholders beyond the financial reporting entity that have a significant effect on the ability of the financial reporting entity to create value. For the purpose of financial reporting, these other entities/stakeholders might be "related parties" but will ordinarily extend further. The purpose of looking beyond the financial reporting boundary is to identify risks, opportunities and outcomes that materially affect the organization's ability to create value. The entities/stakeholders within this portion of the reporting boundary are not related to the financial reporting entity by control or significant influence, but rather by the nature and proximity of the risks, opportunities and outcomes.
>
> (International <IR> Framework, 2013:19–20)

It is worth noting that the boundary of the reporting entity under integrated reporting is coterminous with that under IFRS, in spite of the fact that the focus of integrated reporting is not only the creation of profit, but value conceived in the broader sense.

In the author's view, this further compounds the rather vague definition employed under IFRS. The reasons for this choice are twofold and are explained in the preparatory document of the International <IR> Framework, specifically in the Prototype Framework released in November 2012. These reasons relate to the nature of the primary audience for an integrated report, i.e. investors, and to the acknowledgment of the centrality of the information contained in the financial statement.

> Central to the reporting boundary for <IR> purposes is the financial reporting entity. This is because:
> - It is the financial reporting entity that providers of financial capital, the primary audience for an integrated report, invest in and therefore need information about
> - Using the financial reporting entity enables the information in the financial statements to serve as an anchor or point of reference to which the other information in the integrated report can be related as appropriate.
>
> (Prototype Framework, 2012, para. 5.13:42)

To put it another way, a sort of 'investee entity' concept emerges, i.e. an entity of interest to investors, which clearly differentiates the purpose of an integrated report from that of a sustainability report.[3]

This is explained by the former Technical Director for Framework Development of the IIRC:

> I was involved in the early stages of the GRI boundaries project (2004) and was on their Technical Advisory Committee and then GSSB from inception (2005) till December last year. So when we did the Framework, I had the GRI perspective in my head, but also some earlier thoughts I had input to the Boundaries project: in particular, the concepts from accounting standards of (a) a reporting/economic entity, (b) joint ventures, (c) equity reporting, and (d) related parties. *An integrated report needs to tie to the financial statements much more closely than does a sustainability report, so it made sense to quote explicitly anchor the <IR> boundary to the financial reporting entity* (more so than does GRI, I think), *and expand it as appropriate in the circumstances.* We used the term 'risks, opportunities and outcomes' to do this.
>
> (Interviewee B, former Technical Director for Framework Development, IIRC)

When defining 'value', the IIRC does not explicitly advance a definition of 'impact' or of 'value' but of 'value creation', which relates to "the process that results in increases, decreases or transformations of the capitals caused by the organization's business activities and outputs" (International <IR> Framework, 2013:33).

3.3 EU Directive no. 95/2014 on Non-Financial and Diversity Information

EU Directive no. 95/2014 on Non-Financial and Diversity Information does not differ broadly from the approaches noted above. Consistent with integrated reporting, it borrows the financial reporting concept of the reporting entity by requiring that entities to be included in the boundaries of reporting should be based on the requirements of IAS and IFRS. The related EU Guidelines on Non-Financial Reporting issued in June 2017 are even more ambiguous, as they do not indicate how the boundaries should be set at all. The (non-) definition of what is value follows from these approaches. Value is not defined: the only references made are to the concepts of 'impact' ('impact of the undertaking's activity'/'impact of businesses on society', similar to the sustainability frameworks and standards) and 'value chain'. However, for the argument here, it is worth pointing out that member states have implemented this requirement in different ways. In Italy, for example, the related law requires an initial inclusion of entities according to IAS/IFRS, and then those which are not considered 'material' to understanding the group performance can be excluded.

3.4 Conclusion

The aim of this Chapter has been to provide an overview of the main changes that have occurred in the identification and definition of reporting boundaries in the sustainability, 'value creation' and integrated areas, as indicated in the guidelines, frameworks and standards that have been issued by the key organisations operating in these fields. From the analysis of these documents and the interviews conducted with the principal representatives of these standard setters and framework developer organisations, it appears quite clear that, with the exception of a few cases, the trend for the definition and identification of reporting boundaries has been to adopt concepts used in financial reporting. To put it differently, the notion of reporting boundary has been 'transplanted' from the financial to the non-financial, even though with a new addition, represented by the concept of materiality.

Notes

1 Disclosure of Scope 3 may imply challenges due to data quality and availability as, as previously described, it refers to the indirect emissions in the value chain (upstream and downstream).
2 Exception is represented by GHG emissions associated with investments. Data challenges and existing accounting guidance render the use of GHG emissions difficult. The Task Force has decided to substitute it with weighted average carbon intensity metric (Recommendations of the Task Force on Climate-related Financial Disclosures, 2017:36).
3 As recently acknowledged also by the Corporate Reporting Dialogue in the so-called Landscape Map, the purpose of the International <IR> Framework is to "help organizations explain to providers of financial capital how they create value over time", while the aim of sustainability-focussed guidelines and standards, such as GRI and SASB is to respectively "enable all organizations – regardless of size, sector or location – to report the sustainability information that matters" (GRI) and to "help public corporations disclose material sustainability information in mandatory SEC filings, such as the Form 10-K and 20-F (SASB)" (The Landscape Map, http://corporatereportingdialogue.com/landscape-map/).

Bibliography

Accounting for Sustainability Project (A4S) (2017), *Essential guide to social and human capital accounting* (A4S: London). (https://www.accountingforsustainability. org/social-and-human-capital)

Climate Disclosure Standards Board (2012), *Climate change reporting framework – Advancing and aligning disclosure of climate change-related information in mainstreams reports*, Edition 1.1. (https://www.cdsb.net/sites/cdsbnet/files/cdsb_ climate_change_reporting_framework_edition_1.1.pdf)

Climate Disclosure Standards Board (CDSB) (2014), *Proposals for boundary setting in mainstream reports*.

Climate Disclosure Standards Board (CDSB) (2015), *CDSB framework for reporting environmental information and natural capital.* (https://www.cdsb.net/sites/cdsbnet/files/cdsb_framework_for_reporting_environmental_information_natural_capital.pdf)

EU Directive no. 95/2014 on *Disclosure of non-financial and diversity information by certain large undertakings and groups.*

EU Guidelines (2017) on *Non-financial reporting (methodology for reporting non-financial information).*

Federal Ministry of Economics and Labour (2004), *Intellectual capital statement – Made in Germany Guideline.* (http://www.akwissensbilanz.org/Infoservice/Infomaterial/Leitfaden_english.pdf)

Global Reporting Initiative (GRI) (2002), *Sustainability reporting guidelines* (G2 guidelines) (Author: South Africa). (https://www.epeat.net/documents/EPEATreferences/GRIguidelines.pdf)

Global Reporting Initiative (GRI) (2003), *GRI project fact sheet.*

Global Reporting Initiative (GRI) (2005), *GRI boundary protocol* (Author: Amsterdam). (https://www.globalreporting.org/resourcelibrary/GRI-Boundary-Protocol.pdf)

Global Reporting Initiative (GRI) (2006), *Sustainability reporting guidelines* (G3 guidelines)(Author:Amsterdam).(https://www.globalreporting.org/resourcelibrary/G3.1-Guidelines-Incl-Technical-Protocol.pdf)

Global Reporting Initiative (GRI) (2013), *Sustainability reporting guidelines* (G4 guidelines)(Author:Amsterdam).(https://www.globalreporting.org/INFORMATION/G4/Pages/default.aspx)

Global Reporting Initiative (GRI) (2016), *GRI standards* (Author: Amsterdam).

Global Reporting Initiative (GRI) (2016), *GRI 103: Management approach* (Author: Amsterdam). (https://www.globalreporting.org/standards)

Greenhouse Gas Protocol (GHG) (2001), *Greenhouse gas protocol – A corporate accounting and reporting standard* (Author: Geneva).

Greenhouse Gas Protocol (GHG) (2004), *Greenhouse gas protocol – A corporate accounting and reporting standard* (Author: Geneva). (http://www.ghgprotocol.org/corporate-standard)

International Integrated Reporting Council (IIRC) (2012), *Prototype framework* (Author:London).(http://integratedreporting.org/wp-content/uploads/2012/11/23.11.12-Prototype-Final.pdf)

International Integrated Reporting Council (IIRC) (2013), *International <IR> framework* (Author: London). (http://integratedreporting.org/resource/international-ir-framework/)

Sustainability Accounting Standards Board (SASB) (2014), *Automobile sustainability accounting standards.* (http://www.sasb.org/wp-content/uploads/2014/09/TR0101_ProvisionalStandard_Automobiles.pdf)

Sustainability Accounting Standards Board (SASB) (2017), *Conceptual framework.* (https://www.sasb.org/wp-content/uploads/2017/02/SASB-Conceptual-Framework.pdf)

Task Force on Climate-related Financial Disclosure (2017), *Recommendations of the task force on climate-related financial disclosures.* (https://www.fsb-tcfd.org/)

World Intellectual Capital/Assets Initiative (WICI) (2016), *WICI intangibles reporting framework version 1.0* (Author: Tokyo). (http://www.wici-global.com/wp-content/uploads/2016/09/WICI-Intangibles-Reporting-Framework_ver-1.0.pdf)

4 From theory to practice

Reporting boundaries from financial to integrated reporting and their professional implications

Following the prescriptions proposed by the standards, frameworks and guidelines for the setting of reporting boundaries in financial and non-financial reporting, the aim of this Chapter is primarily to highlight the main approaches adopted by companies in their organisational practice. Indeed, as maintained in comparative law with reference to constitutional law, there is a difference between law as written and presented in formal documents and law in practice, that is the way in which rules are adopted (Horwitz, 2009; Zambon and Girella, 2016). An analysis of how companies effectively implement the above-described documents and the challenges encountered in doing so contributes to a better understanding of their potential use and evolution. The Chapter presents five case studies which can be seen as exemplary, but not necessarily exhaustive, of the main trends that characterise current practice evidence. The analysis is based on company documents (mainly annual, sustainability and integrated reports) as well as interviews with representatives from the companies responsible for the reporting process. The Chapter then examines two themes that are particularly sensitive for professionals in their assessment of reporting boundaries – the 'reporting entity' and 'materiality'.

4.1 From sustainability to integrated reports: maintenance or change of reporting boundaries?

As illustrated in the previous section, the boundary setting mechanisms in non-financial reporting indicated by the main standard setters as well as the organisations responsible for developing frameworks and guidelines all rely on one main principle despite their many apparent differences: the recognition of financial reporting as the main reference point.

However, in investigating the approaches adopted by preparers internationally, especially in the transition from sustainability practices to integrated reports, they appear quite diverse. Some preserve the existing reporting boundaries for sustainability reporting, while others decide to change them.

70 *From theory to practice*

One example which reflects the former way of reasoning is represented by Unicredit. Established in 1998 as a result of a merger of several Italian banking groups and with the head offices located in Italy, it is a global banking and financial services company. The organisation's journey towards sustainability began almost 20 years ago. Indeed, "sustainability is the essence of its business" (Unicredit webpage, www.unicreditgroup.eu/en/a-sustainable-bank/sustainability-reporting.html). More recently, the choice was made to adopt a more integrated approach and they have released an integrated report since 2014. Despite this shift in the reporting form (from a sustainability to a 'value-creation' based one), the organisation has continued to set the boundaries of its reporting by mainly relying on sustainability concepts, even though alignment is made with the consolidated reports as follows:

> The reporting boundaries include 15 countries where the Group has significant operations [. . .] However, this year Turkey has been excluded from the scope of the report, in line with the Consolidated Reports and Accounts of UniCredit. The scope of the report for figures regarding staff and the calculation of the Value Added corresponds to the Consolidated Reports and Accounts 2014, unless otherwise indicated.
> Any conditions that may limit the scope of this data are clearly disclosed throughout the reports.
> (Unicredit Integrated Report, 2014:2)

In the last edition of the integrated report, a more explicit reference is made to the documents followed in order to set the boundaries, namely the GRI G4 Guidelines and the GHG Protocol. However, these remain related to the sustainability arena. As the Unicredit 2016 Integrated Report states:

> Specifically, the figures and information relating to Scope 1, Scope 2 and Scope 3 of Greenhouse Gas Emissions (GHG) have been prepared in accordance with the GRI-G4 Guidelines and 'The Greenhouse Gas Protocol: A Corporate Accounting and Reporting Standard (Revised Edition, 2004)'. [. . .] The reporting boundaries include 14 countries where the Group has significant operations. [. . .] This year Ukraine is not included in the reporting boundaries following the sale of the Group's stake in the Public Joint Stock Company Ukrsotsbank and its subsidiaries, which took place in October 2016.
> (p. 2)

Compared to the practice undertaken before implementing <IR>, when the company was releasing a sustainability report, it is possible to see that no major changes have been made. This can be seen in the following extract from the 2013 Sustainability Report:

> The reporting boundaries include 15 countries where the Group has significant operations [. . .] With respect to 2012 Report, we report that Kazakhstan exited the reporting boundaries, as a consequence of the sale of the companies operating in this country. As in previous reports, the final section of the Supplement summarizes our principal activities and sustainability performance in Turkey, which is not included in the reporting boundaries.
> Unless otherwise noted, the data related to our workforce and to generated added value corresponds to information provided in our 2013 Consolidated Reports and Accounts. Any conditions that may limit the scope of this data are clearly disclosed throughout the report.
> (Unicredit Sustainability Report, 2013:2)

Other organisations take quite a different approach. Set up in 1863, Solvay is a Belgian chemical company based in Neder-Over-Heembeek (Brussels) whose products "serve diversified markets worldwide, from consumer goods to energy, with one main aim – to improve quality of life and customer performance" (Solvay website, www.solvay.com/en/company/about-solvay/our-company/index.html). Similarly to Unicredit, its path towards sustainability has been quite longstanding, starting almost ten years ago with the publication of a sustainability review and prospects and sustainability indicators progress reports as complementary to annual reports. Since then they have reported sustainability information mainly according to GRI Guidelines and the GHG Protocol.

In 2016 the organisation decided to take a step further and to prepare an integrated report aimed at communicating its commitment towards economic and sustainability issues and its intent to move its attention towards value creation in the medium and long term. As maintained by the Chairman and the CEO of the organisation "this Annual Report has become a more integrated report, aimed at showing our commitment to jointly controlling our economic performance and our sustainable development results. We have defined the domains in which we want to progress and have set ten-year objectives for measuring that progress" (Solvay Integrated Annual Report, 2016:6).

With reference to setting of reporting boundaries, the approach undertaken by the organisation in the development of an <IR> can be said to have evolved considerably compared to the approach previously adopted for the sustainability report. First of all, it has implied a change in the process from a 'silo' approach towards a more 'integrated' approach:

> There have been important changes in the identification of reporting boundaries/scope with the transition to integrated reporting. Before

moving to integrated reporting, each main function had its own scope and boundaries definition and its own dashboard:

- Finance using a financial materiality definition: consolidation if above a certain threshold of turnover or assets;
- Environment looking at production sites where we have operational control (financially consolidated or not);
- Safety looking at sites where we have operational control.

(Interviewee C, Deputy Chief Sustainability Officer, Solvay)

This passage has affected the organisation in three main respects. First of all, in transparency terms: the alignment to external standards has clearly led the organisation to respond more directly and comprehensively to stakeholders' information needs, which previously have sometimes been overlooked. This has in turn led to the necessity to balance and connect information (and departments) that until then have been conceived of as sharply different:

> The first step to sustainability reporting, was to align to external standards (GRI). Before that, as many companies, we were reporting on what we wanted to report on, not necessarily on what our stakeholders wanted to know about. This sounds like a limited change, but it may imply important changes in vocabulary, or presentation of information. Example: when you have a 'Health, Safety and Environment' department, they expect to see their reported information in one section of the report, not to see 'Environment' in an Environmental Performance section of the report, and 'Health and Safety' in a Social Performance section of the report, together with other Human Resources performance figures.
>
> (Interviewee C, Deputy Chief Sustainability Officer, Solvay)

Thirdly, the 'system-based' approach that characterises <IR> has also influenced the need to orientate the organisation towards a more 'financial reporting scope', for 'pragmatic' reasons relating to the type of information used by analysts in order to assess performance, and to the rigidity that is implicit in the financial accounting system:

> The second step, with the evolution towards integrated reporting, was to push all departments to align on financial reporting scope and boundaries. We did this first because we see that analysts are cross-linking performance figures, computing ratios like (greenhouse gas emissions

per value added, or per revenue), or (EBITDA per employee), and second, because if we have to use one common scope and boundary, well, finance has less degrees of freedom than other corporate functions.
(Interviewee C, Deputy Chief Sustainability Officer, Solvay)

This process obviously encountered many difficulties, one of which has been related to the different 'objects' of focus of sustainability and financial reports. As previously described, while financial reporting focusses the setting of reporting boundaries around the concept of legal entity, sustainability reporting takes into consideration the whole value chain which can also imply measurement discrepancies:

It was not easy, one difficulty for example being that finance looks at legal entities, not at sites, when safety or environment looks at business units and sites, not legal entities, and sometimes their reporting software was not set up to add 'legal entities' as a reporting dimension or filter. This also meant that we would not be 'recomputing a base year' for GHG emissions but rather detail variation of emissions: organic growth, specific projects, scope changes, methodology changes.
(Interviewee C, Deputy Chief Sustainability Officer, Solvay)

4.2 From annual to integrated reports (through intellectual capital): distance from and convergence to financial reporting boundaries?

A more singular approach has been adopted by those (German) organisations that have implemented the Guideline issued by the Federal Ministry of Economy and Labour for the preparation of an intellectual capital statement. One case which embodies this approach is Energie Baden-Württemberg AG (EnBW), a publicly traded electric utilities company headquartered in Karlsruhe (Germany). This company decided in 2005 to start reporting on intellectual capital:

We have set ourselves the target of becoming number one in knowledge management in order to ensure the best possible support for and development of the potential of our people (Vision No 10). The goal is to specifically gear existing internal intangible potential to future requirements and thus to pave the way at an early stage for sustainable success.
(EnBW Annual Report, 2005:124)

Even though this makes no explicit reference to reporting boundaries, the indications that 'system boundaries' would be set as a step-by-step process (as suggested by the Guideline) have been followed and the focus was placed on relevant companies in the value-added chain: "We have focused on the electricity business segment and have prepared company-specific knowledge balance sheets in the five most important operating companies along the value-added chain" (EnBW Annual Report, 2005:124). The company has continued to report on this type of information according to the Guideline until 2011. Interestingly, since 2010, the approach for the definition of reporting boundaries has evolved further and has been transformed into an 'alternating approach at segment level':

> The intellectual capital statement is prepared on an alternating basis: in years ending with an odd number it is prepared by the companies in the electricity segments and in even years at companies in the gas segment and the service companies. The results of the current year and of the prior year are consolidated in a group-wide summary [comprising the results of the intellectual capital statement at 14 group entities]. This alternating approach at segment level is primarily related to the speed of change with respect to development of intellectual capital.
> (EnBW Annual Report, 2011:74)

With the implementation of integrated reporting in 2014, the boundaries (or limits as they are referred to in the report) have been aligned to those of the consolidated accounts: "The reporting limits for the nonfinancial performance indicators correspond to the scope of consolidation for the financial reporting, unless otherwise stated" (EnBW Report, 2014:3).

4.3 The hybrid approach

Another example of the main trends in boundary setting is represented by the hybrid approach. As noted in the CDSB Discussion Paper (2015), some organisations explicitly refer to it in the reporting boundary section of their reports. This approach mainly relies on a combination between the indications provided by the extant frameworks, standards and guidelines as well as some 'homemade' organisational procedures. One organisation that has adopted it is BT, one of the leading communications companies, serving the broadband, phone, TV and mobile needs of customers in the UK and in more than 170 countries worldwide.

According to CDSB and the GHG Protocol, BT stated in its 2011 Carbon Emission Statement that a hybrid approach was adopted in setting the organisational boundaries:

Both the CDSB and GHGP allow a company to define the organisational boundaries for carbon reporting according to definitions of "equity share", "financial control" or "operational control". The CDSB and UK Government guidance both recommend use of the "financial control" approach.

Taking the financial control approach would omit most of our buildings which would not be a proper reflection of our business. Therefore, to give the most representative footprint for BT we take a hybrid approach. In essence we report on the emissions associated with energy that we buy or generate worldwide. Where the energy is provided by landlords as part of a full service contract we have not included these emissions. We take a consistent approach where we are the landlord. We do not report on countries that have never reached 250MWh per annum electricity use, nor where we do not have a controlling interest in any Joint Ventures or partnerships.

(BT Carbon Emission Statement, 2011:3)

4.4 A new dimension of the hybrid approach: the inclusion of the United Nations' Sustainable Development Goals

In terms of the hybrid approach, the inclusion of the United Nations' Sustainable Development Goals (SDGs) embodies a new frontier in the process of setting reporting boundaries.

An organisation that has recently adopted this methodology is SAP, probably one of the most well-known IT organisations in the world. Based in Walldorf (Germany), it began to move towards integrated reporting quite a long time ago, releasing its first report according to the International <IR> Framework in 2012.

A mixed approach was adopted in identifying the material topics and their boundaries using GRI G4 Guideline, as well as SASB, the IIRC Framework and the United Nations' Sustainable Development Goals (SDGs):

> When identifying our key topics and their boundaries, we looked first at areas related to our operations and supply chain. Second, we looked at topics related to how our software can help our customers contribute to the achievement of the SDGs.
>
> (SAP Integrated Report, 2016:224)

Interestingly, this approach has not been restricted only to the materiality process, but has been extended to the overall boundary setting mechanism of the organisation: "Our boundaries take two different perspectives: SAP as a company, which includes all our legal entities and operations and supply chain, and SAP as a solution provider enabling our customers" (SAP Integrated Report, 2016:247). This is consistent with the views advanced during the United Nations Conference on Trade and Development. According to some of the panellists, consolidation has an aggregating power that allows for better monitoring of SDGs and, therefore, an alignment between the reporting boundaries of the SDGs and those prescribed by IFRS should be made:

> Consolidation rules play an important role in the process of aggregating data from the company to the corporate level, thus having an impact on the link between corporate reporting and monitoring achievement of the Goals. [...] The reporting boundaries for Sustainable Development Goal indicators should be consistent with the boundaries used in the IFRS Conceptual Framework.
> (UNCTAD International Accounting and Reporting Issues, 2016 Review)

In addition, it is in line with the reasons that has led SAP to adopt integrated reporting:

> We wanted to use integrated report to drive sustainability and integrated thinking into the organisation. [...] We wanted to put pressure on SAP to integrate sustainability and foster collaboration amongst departments [...] Once you have an integrate report there is no way back.
> (Interviewee D, Director Sustainability, SAP)

And on the specific point of SDGs, they have started to be seen as fundamental along with this commitment towards sustainability and, thus, integrated reports:

> Along with those different frameworks, we look at the SDGs framework as the relevant one. [...] As solution provider and consumer enablers in the market, we wanted to help customers to be in line with them. We could have not done that with an annual report and a sustainability report.
> (Interviewee D, Director Sustainability, SAP)

4.5 Development of the reporting entity concept[1]

As previously observed, within the financial arena the investigation of the concept of reporting boundaries is related to other fundamental notions that underpin financial reporting – it is a construction that has no real-world analogue. The reporting entity does not necessarily equate with the 'firm' or the 'legal entity' but is a notion fashioned by accountants to provide a boundary for reporting (Suojanen, 1954). It developed as a consequence of the growth of the modern corporation where reporting evolved from a holding company reporting its interests in other entities as an 'investment' to dissolving legal boundaries and accounting for a holding company and its subsidiaries as though it were a 'single economic entity'. This was driven by regulation rather than any accounting principles – though principles have been retrofitted to elaborate a 'reporting entity' concept (Nobes, 2014). The impact of agency theory, viewing the entity as a 'nexus of contracts' (Jensen and Meckling, 1976) has continued to erode and make permeable the reporting entity boundary. Similarly, stakeholder theory and the relevance of the relationships beyond contractual ones (Mitchell et al., 2015) has also continued to challenge just where the accountant draws the line of what to include in the financial statements and what to ignore. The analogy used by Sterling (1967) is remarkably accurate in explaining the actions of standard setters in relation to setting 'rules' for the boundary of the entity:

> They wait for a fire and then rush in to put it out. Often the previous set of generally accepted principles proves to be insufficient for the resolution of the crisis. In such cases a new principle is introduced ad hoc, i.e., the practices cannot be explained by the existing principles and thus a new principle is introduced for the specific purpose of explaining the practice.
>
> (p. 96)

In fact, it cannot be overlooked that, in addition to the *ad hoc* standards described above, most of the conceptual developments that have been advanced in relation to reporting boundaries in accounting standards are related to the definition of the reporting entity and standards on the basis for consolidation. Interestingly, this connection is not only at the basis of financial accounting, but can be said to underlie the social sciences in general and especially sociology. The problem of whether 'boundaries' come first and then the (social) entity or vice versa has been in fact widely examined by sociologists. In economics, authors such as Chandler (1992) have acknowledged the legal nature of the entity, in that a firm is:

> a legal entity – one that signs contracts with its suppliers, distributors, employees and often customers. It is also an administrative entity, for if there is a division of labour within the firm or, it carries out more than a single activity, a team of managers is needed to coordinate and monitor

these different activities. Once established, a firm becomes a pool of learned skills, physical facilities and liquid capital. Finally, 'for profit' firms have been and still are the instruments in capitalist economies for the production and distribution of current goods and services and for the planning and allocation for future production and distribution.

(Chandler, 1992:483)

With reference to financial accounting, the IASB only began to look at the reporting entity concepts in 2004 as part of a joint project with the FASB on improving the Conceptual Framework for Financial Reporting, which also included formalising the reporting entity concept. In 2006 the Boards released a document containing their preliminary views on the objective of financial reporting and the qualitative characteristics of decision-useful of financial information. In the Discussion Paper (DP) which followed in May 2008 they acknowledged that neither of the two respective Frameworks include the concept of reporting entity at that time.[2] In the IASB Framework (para. 8) the reporting entity was indeed defined in a very vague way as "an entity for which there are users who rely on the financial statements as their major source of financial information about the entity"; and in the FASB Statements of Financial Accounting Concepts there was no definition of a reporting entity or indications about the manner in which to identify one. Accordingly, in order to avoid situations where the principles-based approach to the definition of reporting entity is ignored by practitioners (Walker, 2007), the Boards suggested in the DP to link the concept of reporting entity to the objective of financial reporting and define reporting entity as a "circumscribed area of business activity of interest to present and potential equity investors, lenders and other capital providers" (p. 18) – which is then not limited to the legal entity. Another aspect that is interesting to note for the argument here at stake relates to the concepts of control and reporting boundary which have also been addressed in the DP. With regards to the former, it has to be noted that in the DP it is stated, probably for the first time, that control can be seen as a synonym of power and in particular the power to direct something (p. 23). This equalisation, they recognise, is adopted also by the Canadian Institute of Chartered Accountants and Belgian accounting legislation. However, it cannot be sufficient. Most of these laws (not only Canadian but also Japanese, Chinese, New Zealand and UK) indeed also refer to the 'benefits obtained from that entity' (which exercise power). Therefore, in the document the Boards undertake the view that the concept of control should include that of power as well as the ability to benefit from it. In relation to the aspect of reporting boundaries, in accordance with the definition of reporting entity and of the objective of financial reporting the Board advances the view that when an entity has control over another entity, the boundary between the two should be disregarded and the two entities defined as a sole reporting entity.

Following the consultation period after the release of the DP, in March 2010 the Exposure Draft was published. In this document, the concept of reporting entity was much more articulated as compared to the one provided in the DP, as it has been defined as:

> a circumscribed area of *economic* activities whose financial information *has the potential to be useful* to existing and potential equity investors, lenders and other creditors *who cannot directly obtain the information they need in making decisions about providing resources to the entity and in assessing whether management and the governing board of that entity have made efficient and effective use of the resources provided.*
> (Exposure Draft *Conceptual Framework for Financial Reporting – The Reporting Entity*, emphasis added)

Indeed, it is possible to note that the concept of 'business activity' has been substituted by that of 'economic activity' and that the (vague) expression 'of interest' has been much more strongly explicated in terms of usefulness for those financial capital providers who cannot otherwise have access to information to make decisions and assess the use of the resources provided. To put it differently, the definition of reporting entity could be seen as being mainly moulded around the principle of decision usefulness and of stewardship of management. These changes were mainly made in view of the comments received by respondents during the consultation period, as they asked to clarify both the term 'business' and in particular if it has to be associated to the one of 'business combinations' in the related IASB and FASB accounting standards and the one of 'interest'. Accordingly, the Boards agreed to select the notion of 'economic' in the former case as it is less restrictive "and is likely to work better when the boards consider how the concepts apply to not-for-profit entities" (ED, p. 13) and to better explicate the notion of 'interest' in the latter one.

In addition to this broader definition, the 2010 ED also clarified that all single legal entities have the potential to be reporting entities, unless it is not possible to objectively distinguish its economic activities from those of another entity. In a similar vein, a portion of a legal entity can be recognised as a reporting entity if it is possible to distinguish its economic activities from the rest of the entity and the financial information provided is useful in the way prescribed by the reporting entity definition.

In relation to consolidated financial statements, the emphasis on control as "the power to direct the activities of that other entity to generate benefits for the controlling entity" was retained, although with a further condition, that is, in order to include entities in the consolidation, the control has to be 'exclusive'. The ED in fact specifies that if there is no individual control of one entity but the power is shared amongst two or more entities, none of them would present information on a consolidated basis. Along the same reasoning, the notion of 'significant influence', which was originally advanced in the 7th Directive, has been excluded as a determinant of control in that it is not 'exclusive'. Furthermore, similarly to the DP, the control of an entity has been retained as a determinant for the reporting boundary.

Despite these advances, from the late of 2010s the IASB and the FASB have suspended their joint project on the Conceptual Framework including work on the reporting entity concept, until 2012. When the IASB restarted its Conceptual Framework project, without FASB, the intention of the IASB Board was to include the discussion on this topic not in the Conceptual Framework Discussion Paper of 2013 but in the developments of the later Exposure Draft of May 2015. During this phase two other main features related to the notion of reporting entity were raised for discussion by the IASB staff, being whether the boundaries of reporting are determined by both direct and indirect control or by direct control only (Staff Paper on Reporting Entity – General, May 2014) and the perspective through which the financial statements should be prepared (Staff Paper on Reporting Entity – Perspective, May 2014). Accordingly, in the Exposure Draft of May 2015 it has been advanced that a reporting entity "is an entity that chooses, or is required to, prepare general purpose financial statements" (ED Conceptual Framework, May 2015, para. 3.11) and that it is not necessarily a legal entity. In addition, the boundary of a reporting entity is determined using the notion of 'control' and in particular either direct control only (that leads to unconsolidated financial statement) and both direct and indirect control (that leads to consolidated financial statement). In the case of an entity which is not a legal entity, the boundary of financial statements have to be set in a way that financial information needed by existing and potential investors, lenders and other creditors who rely on financial statements are provided and that faithfully represent the economic activities of the entity (ED Conceptual Framework, May 2015, para. 3.18). As for the notion of control, it is of interest to note that a definition is not provided with reference to the reporting entity but a reference is made to the definition used with regard to an 'asset'. Control is here defined as "the present ability to direct the use of the economic resource and obtain the economic benefits that flow from it" (ED Conceptual Framework, May 2015, para. 4.17); thus differently from the one provided until now, there is no equalisation with the concept of 'power' but with 'the present ability' and the 'activities' have been explicated as 'economic resources'. The feedback received during the comment period mainly confirmed this approach with a few exceptions related to the notions of 'direct' and 'indirect' control perceived to create confusion, and the perspective from which financial statements are prepared – that is the entity view – whose rationales are not fully clear. In relation to the former, the staff proposed to clarify in the Basis for Conclusions for the Conceptual Framework (still to be released) that 'direct' and 'indirect' control relate to the economic resources and obligations for the related claims but not to the subsidiary and that under the direct control only the entity does not look through the legal shells of the entities it controls while it does so through the 'direct and indirect' control. Similarly, with respect to the latter, the staff proposed to clarify in the Basis for Conclusions that the entity view is nowadays consistent with the reality of entities, with the objective of financial statement being to provide useful information to providers of financial capital broadly conceived and both existing and potential.

4.5.1 The function of the reporting entity concept

The reporting entity concept functions beyond determining the boundary of the consolidated financial statements given the nature of the definition. The scope of the consolidated financial statements are typically dictated by legislation relying on the accounting standards to mark the boundary of those financial statements. The creation of special purpose entities and variable interest entities continue to vex standard setters as they attempt to continue to close structures that remain off balance sheet but resemble what in substance is a control relationship.

Outside of the annual consolidated financial statements, a reporting entity can exist merely because there are users interested in a group of economic activities – for example, combined financial statements (or pro-forma statements) typically prepared for a prospectus and other forms of business combinations such as business combinations under common control. In these cases, the principles are much less clear, particularly when it comes to measurement. The debate continues whether it is appropriate to apply fair value in these circumstances given the uplift in values (EFRAG, 2011). Importantly, there are issues for the reliance users can place on such financial statements which is addressed in the next section.

4.6 The reporting boundary and the auditor

Traditionally, the external auditors' statutory role has been to report on the financial statements. As forms of non-financial reporting have grown, there has been increasing interest in assurance being provided on these reports. Most of that assurance is provided on a limited basis (WBCSD, 2016), but the financial statement auditor is required to check that non-financial information in the financial filing is consistent with the financial statements. Those responsibilities have now been extended in the EU with the passage of the Non-financial Reporting Directive. As Client Earth (2017) notes:

> Following recent changes to the law, in addition to this requirement, auditors must now also consider and provide assurance that this other information is not just consistent with the accounts, but has itself been prepared in accordance with applicable legal requirements and is free from material misstatements.
>
> (p. 16)

The permeability of the reporting entity boundary and its continual redefinition highlights the degree of judgement involved in decisions about where the reporting entity's reporting should end. It is further complicated by the different reporting frameworks and principles invoked to make those decisions.

4.7 Materiality and stakeholders

4.7.1 The concept of materiality

A principal objective of the financial reporting process is to aggregate and summarise information to a level that enables users of reports to make and assess economic decisions. Whilst much of the process is a mechanical one, deciding what to report (and what not to report) is based on employing a concept of relevance – materiality. Materiality is essentially a judgement process (ICAS, 2012) that is used to select and reject what is eventually included in the financial statements and other general purpose reports such as annual reports, integrated reports and sustainability reports. Materiality is perhaps the most pervasive and enduring concept in financial reporting. As Solomon's observed 'materiality' has been widely used by accountants but it does not always mean the same thing (Solomons, 1986). It seems somewhat obvious that reporting should be underpinned by a judgement that focuses on what is relevant (and excluding what is irrelevant); however, as that involves a judgement by the preparer, it is not so clear cut. That judgement is both entity-specific and timebound – what is considered relevant to report today about an oil and gas company is different to what the position was over a century ago when preparing an income statement was seen as a radical and unhelpful step (Napier, 1996). Debates have continued in parallel with the evolution of financial reporting about how to apply materiality (Slack and Campbell, 2016). It is an area where standard setters are continually asked to provide further guidance (see IASB, 2017).

The growth of non- or extra-financial reporting has intensified the debate on how materiality judgements should be made. 'Materiality', according to the IASB, is an entity-specific aspect of the qualitative characteristic of 'relevance' (IASB, 2010c). For the purposes of the financial statements, quantitative thresholds are typically applied to determine what is material based on a percentage (5–10% of a relevant total) though standard setters have continued to argue that professional judgement needs to be exercised (IASB, 2017). When it comes to qualitative information or quantitative information for which there is not a direct relationship with a financial statement total (such as KPIs), the application of materiality remains elusive (e.g. EFRAG, 2012). Central to these debates has been establishing 'material to whom?'. Financial reports are generally prepared for investors (IASB, 2010a) so information is material if it is relevant to investors in making or assessing decisions about the allocation of resources.

Materiality as a concept is relational – it only has meaning when considered in the context of an ultimate user. Staubus, in his seminal work published in 1961, sharpened the focus of reporting on being 'decision-useful' to a specific group of stakeholders – namely investors (Zeff, 2013). Staubus (1971) noted:

> When we recognize the investor group as a major consumer of the accountant's product, and, at the same time, realize that the product is information we quickly find ourselves facing the question "What information does the investor need?". This query cannot be answered without considering the uses to be made of the information. Then, by taking into account the measurement aspect of accounting, we quickly arrive at the conclusion that the major objective of accounting is provide quantitative economic information that will be useful in making investment decisions.
>
> (p. viii)

This thinking has become the bedrock of financial reporting and how the object of reporting is to satisfy the decision-usefulness of information for investors.

While seemingly straightforward, standard setters such as the IASB and FASB have anchored financial reporting to this basic tenet, which has within it a fundamental flaw that the preparer can know the mind of the investor. It was less problematic when the reporting was essentially comprised of the financial statements and the footnotes that amplified the line items in the financial statements. As the information set has widened to include financial and non-financial information about the business context, deciding what may or may not be relevant to investors has increasingly become problematic and led to the exponential growth in the size of the annual report as what is considered 'relevant' by policy makers continues to extend the boundaries of reporting to include information that may be relevant to investors and other stakeholders.[3]

4.7.2 A babel of definitions

The definition of materiality has remained constant over time until recently when reporting frameworks have emerged that take a broader view of stakeholders beyond satisfying the needs of investors. The IASB defines 'materiality' as:

> Information is material if omitting it or misstating it could influence decisions that users make on the basis of financial information about a specific reporting entity. In other words, materiality is an entity-specific aspect of relevance based on the nature or magnitude, or both, of the items to which the information relates in the context of an individual entity's financial report. Consequently, the Board cannot specify a uniform quantitative threshold for materiality or predetermine what could be material in a particular situation.

Other standard setters have adopted similar definitions of materiality. In the US, materiality has been defined by the Supreme Court in *TSC Industries v Northway Inc.* (1976) as: "a substantial likelihood that the disclosure of the omitted fact would have been viewed by the reasonable investor as having significantly altered the 'total mix' of information made available". Whilst it has some common elements with the IASB's definition, the reasonableness test adds a further dimension and the FASB has been reluctant to codify the legal definition within it standards. The prevalence of other reporting frameworks,[4] such as GRI and Integrated Reporting, has led to various definitions of materiality. The Corporate Reporting Dialogue (CRD) has attempted to explain the definitions employed in eight of the most common frameworks. The ambition was to explore whether convergence was possible, but in the end the CRD catalogued the various definitions drawing out some of the common features. The CRD (2016) concluded: "While each serves different purposes and operates in different contexts, all are definitionally aligned in that material information is any information which is capable of making a difference to the evaluation and analysis at hand" (p. 3). The CRD has merely reinforced that materiality is a relational concept and its definition depends on the end user and their information needs. Through the setting of conceptual frameworks, standard setters establish the parameters of what they believe to be material to end users by employing an extensive due process of consulting with stakeholders to understand what is likely to be relevant to them in making and assessing decisions. For example, the IASB has determined that certain social and environmental factors are not relevant for inclusion in the financial statements, such as the value of human capital or intangibles (outside a business combination), so these are taken out of the frame of what preparers are able to make materiality judgements about. In effect, even though similarities can be found in some common elements of various definitions, the issue centres on how those definitions are applied under each of these frameworks.

4.7.3 Materiality judgements

In practice, materiality is applied in two different ways – normative and empirical. Under IFRS, the preparer is required to make a judgement based on a 'hypothetical' investor and their implied information needs. While there is a process as to how that judgement should be made, which has recently been expanded on by the IASB in Practice Statement 2: Making Materiality Judgements, it remains a test based on the preparer attempting to understand the mind of the investor. This approach is also consistent with the approach in the US in the preparation of the 10K filing and in sustainability reports prepared in accordance with standards issued by the Sustainability Accounting Standards Board – though in the US the application of materiality is less open to judgement as the SEC takes a prescriptive approach to what should reasonably be disclosed in the financial filing. Consistent with that approach, the SASB has prescribed what companies in particular industries should disclose. It is, therefore, a normative-based judgement on 'what the investor should want to know'. Conversely, under GRI 101: Foundation standards (2016), materiality is assessed by considering the economic, environmental and social impact of the entity and their significance to stakeholder decision-making. This is often established empirically by asking stakeholder, typically through a survey, what issues they believe are material and a 'materiality matrix' is developed to help the entity to prioritise what information should be reported. As GRI information is usually reported in a voluntary sustainability report, evidence has shown that this process is not always applied consistently, and it is not always possible to assess how the reporting entity has made its materiality judgement (WBCSD, 2017).

The landscape is further confused by the IASB's definition of materiality being extended beyond the financial statements to narrative disclosures in the financial filing. For example, the IASB, after much deliberation, decided that the definition and application of materiality that had been developed for the financial statements was equally applicable to Management Commentary (IASB, 2010b). This view has been reinforced by regulators (such as the Financial Reporting Council in the UK) which have extended the application of the IASB definition to narrative reporting (e.g. FRC, 2014). How materiality judgements are made by preparers in terms of narrative reporting remains opaque and both regulators and professionals have highlighted the need to improve the relevance of narrative reporting (e.g. FRC, 2017; PwC, 2017). Investors have also indicated that reporting continues to fail to meet their needs and that the debate should not be focused on the quantity of what is reported but its quality (CFA, 2017).

4.7.4 Implications of materiality for the reporting boundary

Materiality not only has implications for what is reported; through its application it can bring transactions and other events within the boundary of the reporting entity. For example, one of the drivers for leasing property, plant and equipment was to shift the risks and rewards of ownership to the lessor and to keep the asset and the liability for lease payments for operating lease arrangements 'off-balance'. IFRS 16 *Leases* has altered that boundary by effectively removing the notion of 'operating leases' and brought leases onto the lessee's balance sheet. Human rights disclosures in narrative reporting have also drawn aspects of the reporting entity's supply chain within the boundary of the reporting entity, recognising a responsibility for externalities created by the reporting entity.

Accordingly, the boundary of the reporting entity continues to be extended and redefined through the application of materiality, drawing in transactions and events that were, under the neo-classical view of the firm, considered to either transfer risks and reward to another party or to be externalities, and for governments and society at large to address through regulation and consumer behaviour. As those 'externalities' are increasingly 'internalised' by the modern corporation, the phenomenon of what is considered relevant continues to make the boundaries of the firm permeable and dynamic. This is not a new phenomenon, as standard setters and financial engineers continually play a game of 'cat and mouse' with regulation, constantly trying to catch up with new financial products that existing accounting standards fail to adequately capture in the financial statements (Sunder, 2016).

For the purposes of sustainability reporting, materiality has for some time been explicitly seen as a means of setting the boundary for what the reporting entity includes within reporting. For example, under GRI 101, for each material topic the 'boundary' is set by considering the needs of stakeholders.

The focus on the relevance of an entity's business model is also serving to shift the emphasis away from considering just those relationships where there is control over another entity to the complex web of stakeholder relationship that the business depends on to create value (Haslam et al., 2015).

4.8 Conclusion

The aim of this Chapter has been to start illustrating how companies effectively identify and define reporting boundaries. In particular, five cases have been examined as exemplary of the main trends that characterise current practice. As a result of these analyses, five different approaches have been outlined. In the shift from sustainability to integrated reports, organisations either maintain or change their reporting boundaries, from annual to integrated reports (through intellectual capital) a divergence first (when information on intellectual capital is reported) and convergence then (when integrated reporting is implemented) have been found. A hybrid approach is also used in order to implement the different frameworks and standards and an innovative hybrid approach that includes the Sustainable Development Goals (SDGs) has also been recently advanced. The Chapter then examined two themes that are particularly sensitive for professionals in their assessment of reporting boundaries. These are the 'reporting entity' and 'materiality'. It can be observed that both of them continue to be critical concepts for reporting. The case of materiality is especially noteworthy, not just because it means 'filtering' information to be reported to exclude information that is not relevant to the end user, but also because also it can in effect redefine what is scoped within the boundary of the reporting entity. The definition of materiality is reasonably straightforward, emphasising the need only to report information that is 'relevant' to the end user. What is problematic is the execution of that judgement in terms of what is likely to be significant to the end user in terms of the purpose to which they want to use the information. For financial reporting there has been a deliberate shift away from assessing the stewardship of resources to a focus on predicting future cash flows, adopting a neo-classical view of the investor's primary interest – the generation of short-term positive cash flows. Contrastingly, for sustainability reporting the emphasis has remained on stewardship over resources and long-term impacts including creating value for a broad range of stakeholders. It underscores the inherent 'logic' and consistency in how materiality should be within a given purpose to which the selection of information is intended.

Notes

1 The following paragraphs have been by written by Mario Abela (Queen Mary University of London, United Kingdom)
   4.5   Development of the reporting entity concept
   4.5.1 The function of the reporting entity concept
   4.6   The reporting boundary and the auditor
   4.7   Materiality and stakeholders

4.7.1 The concept of materiality
4.7.2 A babel of definitions
4.7.3 Materiality judgements
4.7.4 Implications of materiality for the reporting boundary

2 The term has been referred to in the 1980s by Holder (Ball, 1998) but it was originally developed by the Australian Accounting Research Foundation with reference to their project on a conceptual framework for general purpose financial reporting.
3 The EU Non-Financial Reporting Directive (2014) along with other statutory requirements in other jurisdictions have continued to 'blur' the concept of the investor being the primary stakeholder of the annual report (or financial filing in the US) to include information that is likely to be relevant to wider group of stakeholders as the reporting entity's accountability extends beyond describing financial performance. Similarly, investors are increasingly recognising that non-financial information is also decision-useful for investors (CFA, 2017).
4 The Reporting Exchange (www.reportingexchange.com) has identified over 170 reporting frameworks.

Bibliography

Ball, I. (1988), *Definition of the reporting entity*, Australian Accounting Research Foundation, Accounting Theory Monograph No. 8.
BT Carbon Emission Statement (2011), www.btplc.com/Purposefulbusiness/better futurereport/PDF/2011/BT_carbon_accounts_2011.pdf. Accessed on 27 December 2017.
Carbon Disclosure Standards Board (CDSB) (2015), *CDSB Framework for reporting environmental information and natural capital*. London.
CFA Institute (2017), *Global perceptions of environmental, social and governance (Esg) investing the investment*. (https://www.cfainstitute.org/learning/future/Documents/RGB_Digital%20brochure.pdf). Accessed on 27 December 2017.
Chandler, A. D. (1992), What is a firm?: A historical perspective, *European Economic Review*, 36(2–3), pp. 483–492.Client Earth (2017) *Client Earth is Europe's leading environmental law organisation: Climate change and professional liability risks for auditors*.
Corporate Reporting Dialogue (CRD) (2016), *Statement of common principles of materiality of the corporate reporting dialogue*.
EFRAG (2011), *Accounting for business combinations under common control*.
EFRAG (2012), *EFRAG, ANC & FRC discussion paper: Towards a Disclosure framework for the notes*, Discussion Paper.
EnBW Annual Report (2005), www.enbw.com/company/the-group/about-us/publications/download-center/. Accessed on 1 December 2017.
EnBW Annual Report (2011), www.enbw.com/company/the-group/about-us/publications/download-center/. Accessed on 1 December 2017.
EnBW Report (2014), www.enbw.com/company/the-group/about-us/publications/download-center/. Accessed on 1 December 2017.
Financial Reporting Council (FRC) (2014), *Guidance on the strategic report*.
Financial Reporting Council (FRC) (2017), *Annual review of corporate reporting characteristics of good corporate reporting: A single story*.

Global Reporting Initiative (GRI) (2016), *GRI 101: Foundation standards*.
Haslam, C., Tsitsianis, N., Andersson, T., and Gleadle, P. (2015), Accounting for business models and increasing the visibility of stakeholders, *Journal of Business Models*, 3(1), pp. 62–80.
Horwitz, M. J. (2009), Constitutional transplants, *Theoretical Inquiries in Law*, 10(2), pp. 535–560.
ICAS (2012), *A professional judgment framework for financial reporting: An international guide for preparers, auditors, regulators and standard setters*.
International Accounting Standards Board (IASB) (2008), *Preliminary views on an improved conceptual framework for financial reporting – The reporting entity*, Discussion Paper.
International Accounting Standards Board (IASB) (2010a), *The conceptual framework for financial reporting 2010*.
International Accounting Standards Board (IASB) (2010b), *IFRS practice statement management commentary a framework for presentation*.
International Accounting Standards Board (IASB) (2010c), *Conceptual framework for financial reporting – The reporting entity*, Exposure Draft.
International Accounting Standards Board (IASB) (2013), *A review of the conceptual framework for financial reporting*, Discussion Paper.
International Accounting Standards Board (IASB) (2014), *Staff paper on reporting entity – General*.
International Accounting Standards Board (IASB) (2015), *Conceptual framework for financial reporting*, Exposure Draft.
International Accounting Standards Board (IASB (2017), *Making Materiality Judgements – Practice Statement 2*, pp. 1–23.
Jensen, M. C., and Meckling, W. H. (1976), Theory of the firm: Managerial behavior, agency costs and ownership structure, *Journal of Financial Economics*, 3(4), pp. 305–360.
Mitchell, R. K., Van Buren, H. J., Greenwood, M., and Freeman, R. E. (2015), Stakeholder inclusion and accounting for stakeholders, *Journal of Management Studies*, 52(7), pp. 851–877.
Napier, C. J. (1996), Accounting and the absence of a business economics tradition in the United Kingdom, *European Accounting Review*, 5(3), pp. 449–481.
Nobes, C. (2014), The development of national and transnational regulation on the scope of consolidation, *Accounting, Auditing & Accountability Journal*, 27(6), pp. 995–1025.
PricewaterhouseCoopers (2017), *Accountability in Changing Times*.
SAP Integrated Report (2016), www.sap.com/docs/download/investors/2016/sap-2016-integrated-report.pdf. Accessed on 3 November 2017.
Slack, R. and Campbell, D. (2016), *Meeting users' information needs: The use and usefulness of integrated reporting*.
Solomons, D. (1986), The Fasb's conceptual framework: An evaluation, *Journal of Accountancy*, 161(6), pp. 114–124.
Solvay Integrated Annual Report (2016), Accessed on 13 December 2017. www.solvay.com/en/binaries/Solvay_ar16_EN-310315.pdf.
Staubus, G. J. (1971), *A theory of accounting to investors* (Houston, TX: Scholars Book Company).

Sterling, R. R. (1967), A statement of basic accounting theory: A review article, *Journal of Accounting Research*, 5(1), pp. 95–112.

Sunder, S. (2016), *Better financial reporting: Meanings and means*.

Suojanen, W. W. (1954), Accounting theory and the large corporation, *The Accounting Review*, 29(3), pp. 391–398.

Unicredit Integrated Report (2014), www.unicreditgroup.eu/content/dam/unicredit group-eu/documents/en/sustainability/sustainability-reports/2014/2014_Integrated_ Report.pdf. Accessed on 15 December 2017.

Unicredit Integrated Report (2016), www.unicreditgroup.eu/content/dam/unicredit group-eu/documents/en/sustainability/sustainability-reports/2016/2016-Integrated-Report_interactive_13042017.pdf. Accessed on 15 December 2017.

Unicredit Sustainability Report (2013), www.unicreditgroup.eu/content/dam/unicredit group-eu/documents/en/sustainability/sustainability-reports/2013/Bilancio-Sostenibilita-2013-ENG.pdf. Accessed on 15 December 2017.

United Nations Conference on Trade and Development (UNCTAD) (2016), International Accounting and Reporting Issues, 2016 Review. (http://unctad.org/en/pages/PublicationWebflyer.aspx?publicationid=1895)

US Supreme Court (1976), TSC Industries, Inc. v. Northway, Inc., 426 US 438.

Walker, R. G. (2007), Reporting entity concept: A case study of the failure of principles-based regulation, *Abacus*, 43(1), pp. 49–75.

World Business Council for Sustainable Development (WBCSD) (2016), *Generating Value from External Assurance of Sustainability Reporting*. (http://www.wbcsd.org/Projects/Reporting/Resources/Generating-Value-from-External-Assurance-of-Sustainability-Reporting).

World Business Council for Sustainable Development (WBCSD) (2017), *WBCSD reporting matters 2017*.

Zambon, S., and Girella, L. (2016), Accounting theory and accounting practice as loosely coupled systems: A historical perspective on the Italian case (1930–1990), *Financial Reporting*, 1, pp. 95–133.

Zeff, S. (2013), Discussion of 'the objectives of financial reporting: A historical survey and analysis' by Stephen Zeff (2013), *Accounting and Business Research*, 43(4), pp. 328–328.

5 The boundaries in financial and non-financial reporting
A colossus built on shaky foundations?

5.1 Boundaries in financial and non-financial reporting: a comparison

Table 5.1 summarises some initial observations yielded by the comparison between the ways reporting boundaries have been identified and defined in the financial and non-financial reporting arenas.

As previously stated, for company financial reporting it is not completely possible to set the boundaries of reporting in an explicit way. Hence, their definition is strictly related to those aspects that are central to the existence of the organisation, such as the capital it draws to conduct its activity and the relationships it enters into with those actors around it. In looking at the ways these have evolved, it is possible to state that the boundaries of reporting have enlarged in terms of a 'softer' and 'blurred' conceptualisation of the idea of capital (from resources owned by the company to resources controlled with future economic benefits and lastly to shared value amongst various stakeholders). In turn, this has affected the magnitude of actors to be included in the 'value creation' process of the organisation (from shareholders to stakeholders). In particular, the nature of the relationship that the organisation has with its surrounding actors in terms of the cost or distribution of value to be recognised by virtue of this relationship has progressed. For an organisation that owns all the resources, the relations with shareholders determine no cost or liability, but in the passage from the entity perspective to the social/enterprise one, the return to shareholders and the contribution provided by stakeholders is not conceived as a cost, but as value. Similarly, in the shift from the proprietary and entity views to the enterprise/institutional view, surplus is no longer defined as 'profit' but it is possible to detect the emergence of the notion of 'value'. In particular, 'value added' has been identified as the measurement of the flow of output and its division amongst participants in the organisation, broadly conceived (Haller and Stolowy, 1998; Suojanen, 1954). To put it

Table 5.1 Comparison of the definitions of reporting boundaries in financial and non-financial reporting

	FINANCIAL REPORTING		
	Company Financial Reporting		
Conceptual approaches to reporting boundaries	Notion of capital	Relationship with shareholders/ stakeholders	Surplus definition
Proprietary (Sprague, 1907; Hatfield, 1909; Kester, 1917–1918)	Resources owned	Prominence of shareholders in surplus distribution. Financial relations with shareholders determine no cost or liabilities	Proprietor's net worth/Net profit
Entity ('Distributional' – Paton, 1922; 'Institutional' – Staubus, 1959; Li, 1960a, 1960b; Anthony, 1975)	Controlled resources with future economic benefits (e.g. leasing)	Economic entity is prominent vis-à-vis all stakeholders. Surplus distribution to shareholders determines a cost (Staubus, 1959; Li, 1960a, 1960b; Anthony, 1975)	Profit + interests on long-term debt + taxes (Paton, 1922) Profit minus dividends (Staubus, 1959; Li, 1960a, 1960b) = Net profit to the entity Profit minus cost of equity capital (Anthony, 1975) = Net profit to the entity
Enterprise/Institutional Theory (Suojanen, 1954; Ardemani, 1968; Haller and Stolowy, 1998)	Company as a coalition of resources belonging to various stakeholders	Relationships with main stakeholders determine no cost (distribution of surplus)	Value added as measurement of the flow of output and its division amongst participants in the organisation, broadly conceived (Suojanen, 1954)

Group Financial Reporting

Conceptual approaches to group reporting boundaries*	Scope of consolidation – Criteria*				Surplus definition*
Proprietary	Ownership	Legal control (via majority of voting rights) *EU 7th Directive* *IAS 27* *ARB 51*	Substantial control/dominant influence (via legal arrangements) *EU 7th Directive* *IAS 27* *IFRS 11*	Power (through voting rights or contracting arrangements) *IAS 27* *IFRS 10*	Proprietary narrowly conceived: profit measured through proportional consolidation method Parent company theory: profit and equity measured from the majority interest's perspective[1]
Entity (economic: activity/exercise of control) (Moonitz, 1942, 1951)	Actually exercised control (through voting rights)	De facto control (not based on voting rights)	n.a.	[*IFRS 10*: Not clear whether power should be *actually* exercised or have only a nominal/potential nature]	Profit and equity measured from the perspective of the economic entity as a whole

(*Continued*)

Table 5.1 (Continued)

NON-FINANCIAL REPORTING

Conceptual Approaches	Boundaries Identification	Surplus Definition
Sustainability	*GRI G4 Guidelines (2013)*: inclusion of an organisation according to the control/influence concepts of financial reporting, the economic, social and environmental impact, and the materiality principle. *CDSB Framework (2015)*: boundaries are the same as those used for mainstream (financial) reports. In the case of information excluded from the financial reporting boundaries, this should be distinguished from those related to entities that fall within the boundary. *GHG Protocol (2004)*: organisational boundaries defined in relation to the method (equity or control) which has to be selected for consolidating GHG emissions data. Operational boundaries are defined at the corporate level; after that the organisational boundaries are set. The operational boundaries are applied to identify and categorise direct and indirect emissions at each operational level. *SASB Standards*: 'scope of disclosure' represented by the entities consolidated for financial reporting purposes and, in particular, those in which the registrant has a controlling interest, regardless of the size of minority interests. In the case of unconsolidated entities, information should be disclosed to the extent that the registrant considers it necessary for investors to understand the effect of sustainability topics on the company's financial condition or operating performance. *A4S Essential Guide to Social and Human Capital Accounting (2017)*: 'boundaries assessment' is based on a) the identification of the type of organisational decision being made, b) the determination of where the majority and the most relevant impacts and dependencies related to risks and opportunities occur in the value chain, and c) the appropriate time period to be used. 'Materiality' and 'completeness' as complementary concepts.	*GRI G4 Guidelines (2013)*: no definition of value is provided. The notion of 'impact' has various connotations that can refer to: significant economic, environmental and social, positive, negative, actual, potential, direct, indirect, short term, long term, intended and unintended. *CDSB Framework (2015)*: no definition of value is provided. Reference is made to the notion of environmental impacts that are changes in the condition of the environment. Environmental impacts can be positive or negative, direct or indirect, and may manifest themselves as short- or long-term changes in the balance, stock, flows, availability and quality of natural capital. *GHG Protocol (2004)*: no definition of value is provided. *SASB Framework (2017)*: reference to confirmatory and predictive value of information, which can be used to evaluate past performance and for future planning and decision support. *A4S Essential Guide to Social and Human Capital Accounting (2017)*: reference to different types of 'value' (economic, market, etc.), but no sound definition.

Intangibles	*WICI Intangibles Framework (2016)*: It is not necessary that intangibles are owned or controlled by an organisation. Intangibles are resources available for use by an organisation.	*WICI Intangibles Framework (2016)*: value is articulated in two interrelated types: – strategic value (value related to the enhancement of the competitive, market, product, reputation, and/or risk profile of the organisation) – financial value (value linked to the generation of net cash flows over time).
Integrated Reporting	*International <IR> Framework (2013)*: reporting boundaries are based on the financial reporting entity concept and on the risks, opportunities and outcomes that materially affect the organisation's ability to create value.	*International <IR> Framework (2013)*: no definition of value is provided. Value creation defined as the process that results in increases, decreases or transformations of the capitals caused by the organisation's business activities and outputs.
Non-Financial EU Directive	*EU Directive no. 95/2014*: inclusion of entities within the boundaries on the basis of IAS/IFRS. *EU Guidelines on Non-Financial Reporting (2017)*: a company should explain the scope and boundaries of the information disclosed, in particular when certain information relates only to one or several of its segments, or excludes specific segments. No specification of how these boundaries should be set.	*EU Directive no. 95/2014*: no definition of value is provided. Reference is made to 'impact of the undertaking's activity',"impact of businesses on society'. *EU Guidelines on Non-Financial Reporting (2017)*: reference to value chain and impact.

[1] Although the authors are aware that the equity method is typically associated with the proprietary perspective, it has not been here included as it is not a fully-fledged consolidation method, but a valuation method of investments (Nobes, 2002).

* The absence of authors cited for this section of the table is explained by the unfeasibility to directly link the specific theories therein to individual scholars.

Source: The first part of the table dedicated to 'Financial Reporting' has been adapted from Zambon (1996). The second part of the table dedicated to 'Non-Financial Reporting' is author's own elaboration.

differently, with the enlargement of the organisation and the inclusion of actors not only associated with a 'financial contribution', a 'broader' term has been adopted in order to comprehend the diverse nature of 'contributions' which surround it.

With reference to group financial reporting, since the very first conceptualisations, both the proprietary and entity view for consolidated financial statements can be characterised by a strong intertwining of accounting and law. The criteria for determining the scope of consolidation (and the reporting entity) relied on the legal basis and principally on ownership and voting rights. As noted already by Moonitz (1942) "those situations in which control may exist but is not the subject of objective measure" (Moonitz, 1942:237) were excluded. Over the years, this approach has been modified and the criteria broadened. In the proprietary case, 'control' has first taken on a 'substantial' connotation and then a very blurred (and almost vague) one, i.e. 'power'. In the entity view, the presence of voting rights has been excluded. The most likely explanation for this shift is the increased awareness that the reality for many organisations is that it is no longer determined by the mere ownership or legal structure of the entity. In other words, the separation between ownership and control identified by Berle and Means (1932) seems to have continued to be the hallmark influencing the perspective of professional and academic thinking as well as of standard setters. Accordingly, there has been the need, especially for standard setters, to adopt more sophisticated concepts able to encompass the diverse realities that underlie the manner by which value is created. In addition, the shift from the proprietary to entity view has had an impact on the determination of profit, which has been expanded to encompass the change in measurement resulting in moving from the 'proportional consolidation method' to a 'majority interests perspective'.

As for non-financial reporting, it appears that discourses on the identification and definition of reporting boundaries have not focussed so much on the detailed connotation of the concepts of control (apart from the WICI Intangibles Framework and partially the GHG Protocol) or even whether, or the extent to which, the criteria adopted in financial accounting are also appropriate for the non-financial field. This has somehow been taken for granted. As pointed out by Lamont (1992), "most of the boundaries 'have to do with public evaluation of behaviour, with degrees of conformity to social codes, rather than with hypothetical inner states.' We often simply take them for granted and enact them unthinkingly" (Lamont, 1992:37).

What has embodied the main aspect at stake is the 'insert' which has been proposed, which is the concept of materiality. Indeed, it has been recognised in most of the cases, especially for GRI and the IIRC, but also for SASB and A4S, as the key additional element in setting reporting boundaries. However, the definitions of materiality they give suggest differences from that adopted for financial reporting. They explicitly refer to setting the reporting boundaries of the *whole entity*, while in financial reporting it is adopted to define the relevance of the numbers.[1] To put it differently, the concept of materiality has a multifaceted nature (see Chapter 4) and reflects the function that preparers assign to the form of reporting being developed (Lai et al., 2017).

Drawing upon this change in the definition and application of materiality, it is not surprising that in terms of definition of what is value only WICI and SASB explicitly refer to this notion, although a subtle connection can be made between the conceptual approaches of the non-financial world with the conceptualisation of 'value added' proposed by Suojanen with reference to the 'enterprise view'. The other documents relate to a concept of 'impact' or of 'value'. Furthermore, since in both cases no measurement and/or evaluation methods are proposed, a broader identification of the boundaries renders more difficult the definition of what value is.

5.2 The boundaries of financial and non-financial reporting: concluding remarks

The boundaries of the reporting entity are temporary and shifting; they have been defined and redefined as the reporting map is drawn and redrawn. At the margins of those changes the object of reporting mutates in concert with the context within which it takes place. The aim of this book has been to *problematise* the ways in which, and the processes through which, reporting boundaries are identified and defined vis-à-vis the evolution that is occurring in the corporate reporting landscape, and especially in consideration of the emergence of, and momentum gained by non-financial reporting practices. Indeed, despite the peripheral attention given to this topic, particularly in comparative terms, in the author's view it is a crucial one for understanding the dynamics of accounting. The identification and definition of reporting boundaries reveal implications that become fundamental for an in-depth understanding of the ways accounting is conceptualised.

Accordingly, through a review of the discourses that have been advanced by the main constituencies operating in the financial reporting and non-financial arenas as accompanied by the practices experienced by five international organisations, the definitions of reporting boundaries have been investigated and comparatively examined. In order to do so, an innovative interpretative framework based on the combination of the theoretical schemes advanced by Zambon (1996) and Zambon and Zan (2000) with reference to the analysis of consolidated accounts and the concept of 'boundaries transplantation' has been proposed. On the basis of the investigation, it has been possible to advance several other observations. From a 'micro' perspective, although financial and non-financial reporting are different, if not sometimes opposite in nature (as their denomination indicates), the manners in which the reporting boundaries aspect has been addressed can bring them to a sort of 'pragmatic compromise'. In fact, with the exceptions represented by WICI and by the EU Guidelines on non-financial information that do not provide *ad hoc* definitions, most of the non-financial arena (and not only GRI as indicated by previous works) seems to have relied on, and been derived quite extensively from, the financial one. To put it differently, the ways in which reporting boundaries are identified and defined by the GRI, CDSB, IIRC, SASB, GHG Protocol, guidelines, frameworks and standards are mainly based on a 'conceptual transplantation' from the financial field. Applying the concept of 'transplantation' to non-financial reporting, it is found that the language and meaning closely resembles that used in financial reporting.[2] There is one significant difference which has the effect of redrawing the reporting entity boundary: the application of materiality to include broader resources and relationships stretches the perimeter of the reporting entity to include items not recognised within the scope of the financial statements. This way, it appears here clear that, as previously pointed out, in a terminological perspective 'transplantation' is a different notion as compared to 'expansion', 'creolisation' and 'hybridisation'. In addition, drawing upon the examination here undertaken it is possible also to support the view that 'transplantation' can present some differential nuances vis-à-vis the notion of 'borrowing' (Lane Scheppele as cited by Perju, 2012). Indeed, although a proximity and equivalence between the financial and non-financial reporting realms can appear as possible, the 'instillation' of new attributes in the definition and identification of reporting boundaries, as the notion of materiality represents, will undermine the 'unmodified return' of the concept of reporting boundary, which is one of the main aspects that connotes the definition of borrowing.

This difference between the two fields appears even more challenging if we take a look at the decoupling that exists between the notion of scope and boundary and most importantly at the way value is defined and/or measured. Although we can observe that a 'transplantation' has occurred in terms of the definition of what is a 'reporting boundary', it is interesting to note that the same cannot be said with reference to the connotation of what is 'scope' and the manners through which value is defined and measured. In relation to the former, it is possible to note that, with probably the only exception of the proportional method according to which items of income, expenses, assets and liabilities are measured in proportion to the firm's percentage of participation in the venture, this term is adopted in financial reporting as a synonym for boundary. This is not the case in non-financial reporting. Indeed, both GRI and the GHG protocol advance a difference between the two. In GRI's view "scope is distinct from boundaries in that an organisation could choose extended reporting boundaries (e.g., report data on all the organisations that form the supply chain), but only include a very narrow scope (e.g., only report on human rights performance)" (GRI Boundary Protocol, 2005:21). According to GHG Protocol "scope defines the operational boundaries in relation to indirect and direct GHG emissions" (GHG Protocol, 2004:101) and thus refers only partially to boundaries. However, a convergence between the notion of scope and boundary can be found in the GHG Protocol with reference to 'inventory boundary' defined as "an imaginary line that encompasses the direct and indirect emissions that are included in the inventory. It results from the chosen organizational and operational boundaries" (GHG Protocol, 2004:101).

The reasons for these discrepancies can soon be identified as being the legislative requirements they are (or are not) subject to. In financial reporting what is included within the boundaries has to be reported *in toto*, thus representing its scope. In non-financial reporting, and particularly in sustainability, this is not always the case. Accordingly, the 'socio-economic-legal context' as pointed out in Zambon's scheme (1996) is recognised as a relevant aspect to be considered in the comparative analysis of the different nature and forms of reporting practices.

As for the notion of value, it appears to differ quite sharply between the financial and non-financial fields both in the terminological and meaning sense. Furthermore, within the financial and non-financial fields themselves, diverse notions and measurement methods are adopted according to the conceptual approaches through which the value creation process is conceived (Tinker et al., 1982). Differently from what was noted by Carnegie and West (2005), the non-financial reporting field is starting to be able to escape from the boundaries set by conventional accounting through which a monetary value has to be assigned, even though a jurisdictional tension between monetary and non-monetary systems of accountability is yet to be solved.

To put it differently, it can be maintained that, in looking at the ways boundaries are cast, fundamental reflections on what is meant as the object of accounting and its purpose emerged and vice versa.[3] More generally, an 'accounting relativism' can be said to be maintained in the shift from financial to non-financial reporting.

Following this line of thought, in view of the observations advanced above, the interpretative scheme of Zambon (1996) and Zambon and Zan (2000) can be re-drawn in order to better acknowledge the role of boundaries in the evolution witnessed in the corporate reporting system. Accordingly, in the former the boundaries of reporting could be drawn, with reference to financial reporting, in between the accounting model and the users, with the exception of internal users, which will be considered as laying within the boundaries (Figure 5.1). This conceptualisation can be seen to derive from the repeated attempts at 'objectivisation' that this form of reporting has been subject to for decades, and especially since the rise of Anglo-Saxon accounting thought, deriving from economics. By referring to actors that (effectively or assumedly) operate in the market (which is seen as external to the organisation) the financial reporting system assumes, or is thought to assume, an objective, factual dimension of its own. With the full recognition of minority interests (see Chapter 2), and the acceptance of the 'entity view' as a conceptualisation of a 'reporting entity' (see Chapter 4), financial reporting has started to assume a more subjective facet.

With reference to non-financial reporting, both internal and external users are directly included in the boundaries through the materiality determination process (Figures 5.2).

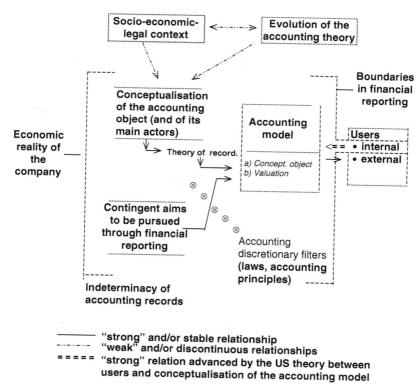

Figure 5.1 The boundaries in financial reporting

Source: Zambon's scheme as adapted by the author.

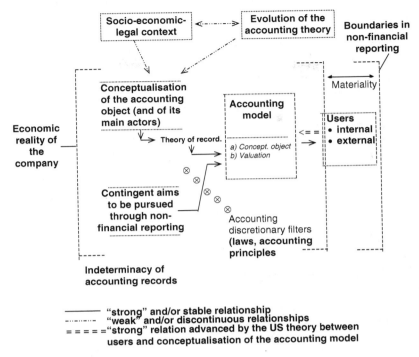

Figure 5.2 The boundaries in non-financial reporting
Source: Zambon's scheme as adapted by the author.

So it can also be stated that the boundary setting mechanism is not meant to draw a rigid, sharp line of distinction and inequality between what is inside and what is outside. This is what Durkheim (1911) refers to as the realm of sacred and of the profane or what is currently known as 'symbolic boundaries' (Epstein, 1992; Lamont et al., 2001; Lamont and Fournier, 1992). The categorisation and 'objectivisation' process seems to fade away – materiality indeed inherently implies judgement – towards a recognition of the role that a broad range of stakeholders can provide in terms of value creation.

To put it another way, there has been a recognition that "our neat and orderly classifications notwithstanding, the world presents itself not in pure black and white but, rather, in ambiguous shades of grey, with mental twilight zones and intermediate essences" (Zerubavel, 1991:71), or what Lamont (1992) refers to as a "zone made up of elements that leave us indifferent and are tolerable" (p. 36).

These perspectives derive from the object, purpose and nature that underlie this new conception of reporting, a conception which is more in line with the 'stakeholder democracy' movement and the 'inclusive capitalism' period that we currently live in:

> For me, an inclusive economic system means extending accountability beyond financial transactions and recognising that society impacts business. [...] An inclusive system seeks to enhance the value to business of all economic, human, social and environmental resources. It builds an understanding of the decisions and trade-offs, made over different time horizons, which impact an organization's strategy and business model.
>
> (Druckman, 2016)

However, it is particularly important to pay attention to two aspects – the reporting entity and the information users. How can we in fact define a 'reporting entity' in the era of non-financial reporting? Is the 'entity view' an acceptable theorisation? Or does non-financial reporting need a new conceptualisation of what is an entity?

Concerns relate also to the nature and effective significance of the information users. Just as users may be 'made up' (Young, 2006) in financial reporting in order to preserve the status quo, non-financial reporting tends towards enlarging the number (and quality) of the stakeholders in order to reflect the logic this type of reporting (especially sustainability reporting) has been created for, i.e. to meet the needs of stakeholders that have previously been omitted from the landscape of traditional financial reporting. To put it another way, the corporate reporting system continues to exist in a vicious circle of what can be defined, to paraphrase a well-known 1985 movie, "desperately seeking users", forgetting that those users (and, if not users per se, their relevance) are often intentionally created simply to preserve the usefulness of this system. At the end of the day, it is not to be forgotten that reporting (and accounting) is human made, and therefore derives from and responds to human logics and vulnerabilities.

In relation to the implications these changes have had on the relationship between measurement and theorisation aspects (Zambon and Zan, 2000), the notion of income measurement is now accompanied by the one of value and the logical correlation between theories of the firm, accounting theories, and income measurement can be seen in both senses. In other words, by looking at the way income or value are defined it is also possible to infer the underlying theory of the firm (Figure 5.3).

In addition, some reasons that underlie the decision of non-financial organisations to 'transplant' the concept of reporting boundary can be offered,

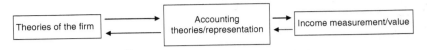

Figure 5.3 Logical correlation between theories of the firm, accounting theories and income measurement in financial and non-financial reporting

Source: author's elaboration.

though a more in-depth investigation will need to be addressed in future works. Indeed, in examining the documents and the results obtained it can be noted that in some cases this can be due to cost-saving motivations (Miller, 2003) or also to reputational/legitimacy ones (DiMaggio and Powell, 1983; Deephouse, 1996; Miller, 2003). As explicitly stated in the GRI Boundary Protocol:

> reporting only on entities within the boundary used for financial reporting may fail to tell a balanced and reasonable story of the organisation's sustainability performance and may fall short of the accountability expectations of users. [. . .] This protocol has aligned its concept of control/influence with financial reporting principles as a baseline [. . .] so as to ensure consistency with financial reporting and facilitate comparability and assurability.
>
> (GRI Boundary Protocol, 2005:9)

More implicitly, these choices can also be seen as the cultural and ideological contradictions that are embedded in written laws in an attempt at:

> wavering between looking forward and looking backward, between a recognition of new beginnings and a wish to express what has always been, between the opportunity to break with the past and the need to build on a foundation of timeless truths [. . .] between declaring or finding fundamental law, on the one hand, and making or creating it, on the other.
>
> (Horwitz, 2009:540)

Given the observations noted above, this book has paved the way for future research examining the complexities, tensions and implications of reporting boundaries in financial and non-financial arenas, the implications that these changes have for professional practice and, ultimately, on the theories of accounting and of the firm. By highlighting the intended and unintended consequences that derive from boundary setting both in theory and in practice, and by providing a comprehensive conceptual framework useful for their in-depth understanding, it has attempted to provide boundaries with the 'visibility' that they need in order to be appreciated it their constitutive role. In so doing, the focus on reporting becomes instrumental for the comprehension of those economic, social and political discourses that otherwise would remain undefined. Similarly to the role assigned to accounting vis-à-vis economics and vice versa (Hopwood, 1992),[4] reporting is recognised the role of reporting is recognised to be to 'operationalise' those discourses that underline it. And the economic, social and political discourses provide reporting with an 'escape route' from being conceived as a mere technical practice and in general mobilise its change.

In providing boundaries with 'visibility', the focus should clearly be on the process rather than on the objects that are separated or unified through boundaries. As previously argued, these objects or, rather, subjects (represented by the shareholders and stakeholders that enter from time to time in the definition of what is value and thus what is an entity and its object) and their relevance are most of the time the result of rhetorical exercises in response to vested interests.

I would therefore agree with Zerubavel (1991), and maintain that:

> In order to make them (boundaries) more "visible," we must suspend our usual concern with what they separate and focus instead on the process by which we cut up the world and create meaningful entities. In short, we must examine how we actually separate entities from one another [. . .] how we draw these fine lines will certainly determine the kind of social (and I would here add accounting and corporate reporting) order we shall have.
>
> (1991:3–4)

To conclude, the ways reporting boundaries are defined and set is a topic which needs to be placed at the centre of accounting, financial and non-financial reporting research, institutional and professional agendas (perhaps on the wave of the motto 'Bringing Boundaries Back Again!' paraphrasing the work of Evans et al., 1985). As this book has observed, reporting 'sits' on boundaries that are fragile and continuously transforming and shifting, a colossus built on shaky foundations.[5] Our task as scholars, and of standard setters, framework developer organisations and professionals is to reinforce those foundations. They still do represent very important parts of reporting. Indeed, reporting cannot function without them (Hopwood, 1992).

Notes

1 A summary of the definitions of materiality adopted by GRI, CDP, CDSB, IASB, IIRC, FASB and SASB can be found in the later outlined 'Statement of Common

Materiality' developed by the Corporate Reporting Dialogue (http://corporate reportingdialogue.com/wp-content/uploads/2016/03/Statement-of-Common-Principles-of-Materiality1.pdf). As for the A4S Guidelines, materiality is defined as "the focus on the issues that have the most significant impact on the organization and its stakeholders" (p. 15).

2 In this respect, one could undoubtedly question whether a sort of betrayal is not made by non-financial reporting at the expenses of financial reporting, considering their quite different nature and aim.

3 The investigation on whether the boundaries (Barth, 1969; Abbott, 1995) or the object come first is not here at stake but will be conducted in future works.

4 As stated by Hopwood (1992), "just as economic discourses can provide a basis for empowering and changing accounting so accounting, in turn, can be implicated in the very construction of a sphere of economic endeavour" (p. 141).

5 "You were observing, O king, and behold a statue, a huge statue of extraordinary splendor, stood before you with a terrible appearance. He had a head of pure gold, chest and arms of silver, belly and thighs of bronze, legs of iron and feet partly of iron and partly of clay. While you were looking, a stone broke away from the mountain, but not by the hand of a man, and went to pound against the statue's feet, which were of iron and clay, and shattered them. Then the iron, the clay, the bronze, the silver and the gold also broke and became like the chaff on the threshing floors of summer; the wind carried them away without a trace, while the stone, which had struck the statue, became a great mountain that filled the whole region." (The colossus built on shaky foundations, Bible, Book of Daniel, II, 31–35, as translated by the author.)

Bibliography

Abbott, A. (1995), Things of boundaries, *Social Research*, 62(4), pp. 857–882.

Anthony R.N. (1975), *Accounting for the cost of interest*. (Lexington, Mass.: Lexington Books-D. C. Heath and Co).

Ardemani E. (1968), L'evoluzione del concetto di impresa e dei sistemi contabili in Italia [The evolution of firm concept and accounting systems in Italy], Rivista dei dottori commercialisti, 3 (May–June), pp. 411–430.

Barth, F. (1969), *Ethnic groups and boundaries: The social organization of culture differences* (New York: Little, Brown).

Berle, A., and Means, G. (1932), *The modern corporation and private property* (New York: Macmillan).

Carnegie, G. D., and West, B. P. (2005), Making accounting accountable in the public sector, *Critical Perspectives on Accounting*, 16(7), pp. 905–928.

Deephouse, D. L. (1996), Does isomorphism legitimate? *Academy of Management Journal*, 39(4), pp. 1024–1039.

DiMaggio, P., and Powell, W. W. (1983), The iron cage revisited: Collective rationality and institutional isomorphism in organizational fields, *American Sociological Review*, 48(2), pp. 147–160.

Druckman, P. (2016), Paul Druckman, CEO of the international integrated reporting council discusses the meaning of inclusive capitalism, *Huffington Post*, www.huffingtonpost.com/inclusive-capitalism/paul-druckman-ceo-of-the_b_8542694.html.

Durkheim, E. (1911), *Les formes élémentaires de la vie religieuse* (Paris: Alcan) [1965. *The elementary forms of religious life*. New York: Free Press].

Epstein, C. F. (1992), Tinker-bells and pinups: The construction and reconstruction of gender boundaries at work, in M. Lamont and M. Fournier (eds.), *Cultivating differences: Symbolic boundaries and the making of inequality* (Chicago: University of Chicago Press).

Evans, P. B., Rueschemeyer, D., and Skocpol, T. (1985), *Bringing the state back in* (Cambridge: Cambridge University Press).

Global Reporting Initiative (GRI) (2005). *GRI boundary protocol* (Author: Amsterdam).

Greenhouse Gas Protocol (GHG) (2004), *Greenhouse gas protocol – A corporate accounting and reporting standard* (Author: Geneva).

Haller, A., and Stolowy, H. (1998), Value added in financial accounting: A comparative study between Germany and France, *Advances in International Accounting*, 11(1), pp. 23–51.

Hatfield H.R. (1909), *Modern accounting*. (New York: D. Appleton & Co).

Hopwood, A. G. (1992), Accounting calculation and the shifting sphere of the economic, *European Accounting Review*, 1(1), pp. 125–143.

Horwitz, M. J. (2009), Constitutional transplants, *Theoretical Inquiries in Law*, 10(2), pp. 535–560.

Kester R.B. (1917–1918), *Accounting theory and practice*, 2 Vols. (New York: Ronald Press).

Lai, A., Melloni, G., and Stacchezzini, R. (2017), What does materiality mean to integrated reporting preparers? An empirical exploration, *Meditari Accountancy Research*, pp. 533–552.

Lamont, M. (1992), *Money, morals, and manners: The culture of the French and the American upper-middle class* (Chicago: University of Chicago Press).

Lamont, M., and Fournier, M. (1992), *Cultivating differences: Symbolic boundaries and the making of inequality* (Chicago: University of Chicago Press).

Lamont, M., Pendergrass, S., and Pachucki, M. (2001), Symbolic boundaries, *International Encyclopedia of the Social and Behavioral Sciences*, 23, pp. 15341–15347.

Li D.H. (1960b, October), The nature and treatment of dividends under the entity concept, *The Accounting Review*, 35, pp. 674–679.

Li D.H. (1960a, April), The nature of corporate residual equity under the entity concept, *The Accounting Review*, 35, pp. 258–263.

Miller, J. M. (2003), A typology of legal transplants: Using sociology, legal history and Argentine examples to explain the transplant process, *The American Journal of Comparative Law*, 51(4), pp. 839–886.

Moonitz, M. (1942), The entity approach to consolidated statements, *The Accounting Review*, 17(3), pp. 236–242.

Moonitz M. (1951), *The entity theory of consolidated statements*. (Brooklyin: Foundation Press).

Nobes C. (2002), An analysis of the international development of the equity method, *Abacus*, 38(1), pp. 16–45.

Paton W.A. (1922), *Accounting theory*. (New York: Ronald Press).

Perju, V. (2012), *Constitutional transplants, borrowing, and migrations*, Boston College Law School Faculty Papers.

Sprague Ch. E. (1907), *The philosophy of accounts*. (New York: published by the author)

Staubus G. J. (1959), The residual equity point of view in accounting, *The Accounting Review*, 34(1), pp. 3–13.

Suojanen, W. W. (1954), Accounting theory and the large corporation, *The Accounting Review*, 29(3), pp. 391–398.

Tinker, A. M., Merino, B. D., and Neimark, M. D. (1982), The normative origins of positive theories: Ideology and accounting thought, *Accounting, Organizations and Society*, 7(2), pp. 167–200.

Young, J. J. (2006), Making up users, *Accounting, Organizations and Society*, 31(6), pp. 579–600.

Zambon, S. (1996), *Entità e proprietà nei bilanci di esercizio* [Entity and proprietary in financial statements] (Padua: Cedam).

Zambon, S., and Zan, L. (2000), Accounting relativism: The unstable relationship between income measurement and theories of the firm, *Accounting, Organizations and Society*, 25(8), pp. 799–822.

Zerubavel, E. (1991), *The fine line* (Chicago: University of Chicago Press).

Name Index

Note: Page numbers in italic indicate a figure, and page numbers in bold indicate a table on the corresponding page.

Abbott, A. 1, 105n3
Afuah, A. 9
Alexander, D. 31
Anderson, G. 13
Andrei, P. 14
Annisette, M. 3
Anthony, R. N. 26, **92**
Araujo, L. 8
Archel, P. 13, 14
Ardemani, E. 26, **92**
Arya, B. 17, 18

Bahnson, P. R. 39
Ball, I. 87n2
Barth, F. 105n3
Baxter, W. 40n1
Bensadon, D. 11, 12
Berle, A. 96
Bhimani, A. 18
Billinger, S. 9
Biondi, Y. 9
Bontis, N. 13
Bourdieu, P. 10
Brusoni, S. 10

Campbell, D. 82
Carlile, P. R. 10
Carnegie, G. D. 99
Chandler, A. D. 77, 78
Chiapello, E. 17
Choudhry, S. 4
Christensen, J. 18
Clark, M. W. 37
Coase, R. H. 2, 7, 8

Deephouse, D. L. 103
DiMaggio, P. 103
Dosi, G. 9
Druckman, P. 102
Durkheim, E. 6, 101

Edwards, P. 2
Eisenhardt, K. M. 10
Epstein, C. F. 101
Evans, L. 4
Evans, P. B. 104
Ewald, W. 16

Fitz-Enz, J. 13
Foucault, M. 4
Fournier, M. 101
Fuller, S. 11

Giannessi, E. 9
Gieryn, T. F. 10
Gillespie, J. 16
Gilmore, T. 10
Girard, R. 18n4
Girella, L. 69
Gowthorpe, C. 14
Grandori, A. 14
Grossman, S. 8

Haller, A. 91, **92**
Hamel, G. 9
Harding, A. 16
Hart, O. 8
Haslam, C. 86
Hatfield, H. R. 26, **92**

Haugen, E. 3
Heracleous, L. 10
Hirschhorn, L. 10
Hopwood, A. G. 104, 105n4
Horwitz, M. J. 69, 103
Hurst, D. K. 9

Jacobides, M. G. 9
Jensen, M. C. 77
Journet, D. 3

Kaboolian, L. 9
Kaspersen, M. 14
Kell, W. G. 27
Kester, R. B. 26, **92**
Kettl, D. F. 9, 10
Kohler, E. L. 37

Lai, A. 97
Lamberton, G. 13
Lamont, M. 7, 17, 96, 101
Lefebvre, C. 11, 12
Leiblein, M. J. 9
Lev, B. 2
Li, D. H. 26, **92**
Lightfoot, K. G. 1, 7
Lin, L. Q. 11, 12
Llewellyn, S. 10
Loasby, B. J. 8
Lopes, A. I. 37

Martinez, A. 1, 7
Marx, K. 6
Massey, D. 10, 11
Means, G. 96
Meckling, W. H. 77
Medjad, K. 17
Meyssonnier, F. 14
Miller, D. J. 9
Miller, J. M. 103
Miller, P. 1
Mitchell, R. K. 77
Molnár, V. 7, 17
Moneva, J. M. 13
Moonitz, M. 26, 27, 37, **93**, 96
Mouritsen, J. 14
Musolf, L. D. 9

Napier, C. J. 82
Nelson, R. 9
Nelson, T. 13
Nobes, C. 11, 12, 77, **95**

Palmié, S. 18n5
Paton, W. A. 26, 37, **92**
Penrose, E. 7, 8
Perju, V. 16, 98
Pesci, C. 14
Pisano, G. 9, 10
Pizzo, M. 37
Popper, K. 10
Pourtier, F. 14
Powell, W. W. 103
Prahalad, C. K. 9

Rahaman, A. S. 17
Richardson, G. B. 7, 8
Roebuck, D. 16
Roos, J. 13

Saccon, C. 11, 12
Santos, F. M. 10
Scheppele, L. 16, 98
Scovill, H. T. 37
Seidman, H. 9
Sin, K. K. 16
Slack, R. 82
Smith, M. 37
So, S. 37
Solomons, D. 2, 82
Sprague, Ch. E. 26, **92**
Star, S. L. 10
Staubus, G. J. 26, 83, **92**
Sterling, R. R. 77
Stolowy, H. 91, **92**
Sunder, S. 86
Suojanen, W. W. 26, 77, 91, **92**, 97

Teece, D. J. 9
Tilly, C. 18n3
Tinker, A. M. 99

Viganò, E. 9

Walker, R. G. 11, 17, 78
Wallerstein, I. 10, 11
Walton, P. 11, 13
Watson, A. 16
Weber, M. 7
West, B. P. 99
Williamson, O. E. 7, 8
Winter, S. G. 9

Xing, L. 16

Young, A. 13
Young, J. J. 102

Zambon, S. 2, 9, 15, 16, 69, **95**, 97, 99, *100*, *101*, 102
Zan, L. 2, 9, 15, 16, 97, 99, 102

Zappa, G. 9
Zarowin, P. 2
Zeff, S. A. 9, 40n1, 83
Zerubavel, E. 101, 104
Zhang, G. 17, 18
Zimmerman, B. J. 9

Subject Index

Note: Page numbers in italic indicate a figure, and page numbers in bold indicate a table on the corresponding page.

AAA *see* American Accounting Association (AAA)
A4S *see* Accounting for Sustainability (A4S)
Accountants International Study Group 38
Accounting for Sustainability (A4S) Project 6, 58–59; Essential Guide to Social and Human Capital Accounting 44, 59; non-financial reporting 59, **94**
Accounting Research Bulletin (ARB) no. 51 32–35, 37, 38, **93**
acquisition date, fair value as of 32, 34, 39
American Accounting Association (AAA) 37
ARB *see* Accounting Research Bulletin (ARB)
Arbeitskreis Wissensbilanz **5**, 62–63
auditor, reporting boundary and 81–82
azienda (business entity) 9

borrowing: boundaries 18n3; notion of 98; transplantation and 16–17
boundaries/boundary: assessment 59; firm 7–9; method of research for reporting 3–5; planetary 1; reporting 1–3; in social management studies 6–11; term 3, 4; transplanting concepts across disciplinary 11–18; *see also* reporting boundaries
boundary transplantation, concept of 2, 15, 16

boundary work 10
BT, reporting boundary 74–75
Business Economics 9

Canadian Institute of Chartered Accountants 78
Caterpillar, COSA of 13–14
CCRF *see* Climate Change Reporting Framework (CCRF)
CDSB *see* Climate Disclosure Standards Board (CDSB)
CERES *see* Coalition for Environmentally Responsible Economies (CERES)
Climate Change Reporting Framework (CCRF) 54
Climate Disclosure Standards Board (CDSB) **5**, 6, 44, 51; discussion paper and framework 51–55; GHG Protocol underlining 53; Greenhouse Gas (GHG) Protocol and 74–75; non-financial reporting **94**
Coalition for Environmentally Responsible Economies (CERES) 45
company financial reporting 25, 26, 40, 91, **92**
control: concept of 12, 28–29; *de facto* 12, 27; GHG definition of 56; interactions between IFRS (10, 11, 12) and IAS (28) *31*; power and 47–48; reporting entity 80–81
Corporate Reporting Dialogue (CRD) 67n3, 84, 105n1

Subject Index

corporate social responsibility (CSR) 14, 17, 52
COSA, business unit of Caterpillar 13–14
CRD *see* Corporate Reporting Dialogue (CRD)
creolisation 17, 18n5, 98
CSR *see* corporate social responsibility (CSR)

Economia Aziendale 9
economics: accounting 100; boundaries in 5, 7–8; business 9; legal entity 77–78
Energie Baden-Wurttemberg AG (EnBW) 73–74
Enron 11, 34
enterprise/institutional theory, of financial reporting 26
entity view of financial reporting 26, 40n1
EU Directive no. 95/2014 on Non-Financial and Diversity Information 66–67, **95**
EU Non-Financial Reporting Directive (2014) 87–88n3, **95**
expansion 2, 9, 17, 98

FAS *see* Financial Accounting Standard (FAS)
FASB *see* Financial Accounting Standards Board (FASB)
FASB of the Interpretation (FIN) No. 46R 35, 36
Financial Accounting Standard (FAS) 94, 33; FAS 141(R) *Business Combinations* 32, 34, 38, 39
Financial Accounting Standards Board (FASB) 6, 25, 40; financial reporting views 32–34; minority interests 38–39; reporting entity 78, 79, 80
financial reporting: boundaries in 97–104, *100*; case of special purpose entities 34–37; comparing company and group **92–93**; comparing to non-financial 91, 96–97; definitions of **92–93**; IASB and FASB views of 27–34; logical correlation of *16*, *103*; proprietary *vs* entity theories 25–27; reporting boundaries and minority interests 37–40
Financial Stability Board 6, 44, 55, 59

German Federal Ministry of Economics and Labour 61, 73
GHG *see* Greenhouse Gas (GHG) Protocol
Global Financial Crisis 11
Global Reporting Initiative (GRI) **5**, 6, 14, 44; GRI Boundary Protocol Project 13, 46–48, 103; GRI guidelines 45–46, 48–50; GRI Standards 50–51; non-financial reporting **94**
Greenhouse Gas (GHG) Protocol 6, 44, 55; corporate accounting and reporting standard 56; *Metrics and Targets* 60; non-financial reporting 56–57, 60, 67n2, **94**; scope defining boundaries 99; underlining CDSB approach 53
GRI *see* Global Reporting Initiative (GRI)
group financial reporting 26, 40, **93**, 96

IASB *see* International Accounting Standards Board (IASB)
IFRS *see* International Financial Reporting Standards (IFRS)
IIRC *see* International Integrated Reporting Council (IIRC)
inclusive capitalism 102
integrated reports: from annual to 73–74; from sustainability to 69–73
intellectual capital (IC) 13–14; intangibles field and 61–62
International Accounting Standards Board (IASB) 6, 17, 25; business combinations in *IAS 22* 31–32; control in *IAS 27* 28, 29, **93**; defining materiality 83, 84; entity view 38; financial reporting views 27–32, 27–34; *IAS 3* 11–12, 38; *IAS 27* 12, 32, 35, 38–39, **93**; reporting entity 78, 79, 80; significant influence in *IAS 28* 30–31, *31*
International Financial Reporting Standards (IFRS) 47; control interactions *31*; *de facto* power 29; *IFRS 3* minority interests 38; *IFRS 10* 12, 14, **93**; control and power 28–29; *IFRS 11* 30, *31*, **93**; *IFRS 12* 30, *31*, 41n3; *IFRS 16* 86

International Integrated Reporting Council (IIRC) 5, 6, 44, 64; IIRC framework 64–66, 67n3; non-financial reporting 95
interviews in person and via Skype 4, 5

knowledge economy 9
knowledge specialisation 10

Landscape Map 67n3
legal transplantation 16
linguistic borrowing 3

map making, notion of 2
materiality: concept of 82–84; definitions of 84–85, 104–105n1; implications for reporting boundary 86; judgements 85–86; stakeholders and 82–86
Member State 40–41n2
mimesis 3, 18n4
minority interests 6, 25, 100; measurement of 34, 36; reporting boundaries and 37–40; size of 58, **94**; treatment of 33, 40

National Greenhouse and Energy Reporting Act (NGER) 13
non-controlling interests (NCI) 32, 34, 37–40
non-financial reporting: boundaries in 97–104, *101*; CDSB (Climate Disclosure Standards Board) 51; CDSB discussion paper and framework 51–55; comparing to financial 91, 96–97; definitions of **94–95**; EU Directive no. 95/2014 on 66–67; Greenhouse Gas (GHG) Protocol 55, 55–57; GRI (Global Reporting Initiative) 45; GRI Guidelines, the GRI Boundary Protocol and GRI Standards 45–51; IIRC (International Integrated Reporting Council) 64; IIRC framework 64–66, 67n3; logical correlation of *103*; reporting practices 44–45; 'value creation'-based approaches to 60–66, 91; WICI (World Intellectual Capital/Assets Initiative) 60; WICI intangibles framework 60–64

orientation postulate 9, 40n1
ownership 8, 30, 35; concept of 12; controlling financial interest 32–34; cross-ownership 52; group financial reporting 93; legal 46, 57, 96; shifting risks and rewards of 86; voting rights and 27, 96

planetary boundaries 1
pooling-of-interests method, financial reporting 32
power 10–12, 27, 76; control and 28, 47–48, 78–80, 96; *de facto* 29; definition of 29, 34; entity control 35, 36, 56; group financial reporting 93; of investor 29; of reporting organisation 55; rights and 29; term 55; voting 27, 28, 30
proprietary view of financial reporting 26, 27, 40n1
purchase method, financial reporting 32, 34

Recommendations of the Task Force on Climate-related Disclosures 6
relationships, boundary setting of 8–9
reporting boundaries 1–3; from annual to integrated reports 73–74; auditor and 81–82; comparison of financial and non-financial 91, 96–97; concept of 16; definition of 25; development of reporting entity concept 76–81; financial and non-financial 14, 97–104; hybrid approach to 74–75; hybrid including United Nations Sustainable Development Goals 75–76; implications of materiality for 86; intellectual capital and 73–74; materiality and stakeholders 82–86; method of research for 3–5; minority interests and 37–40; *see also* boundaries/boundary
reporting entity 18n1; control of boundaries 80–81; definition of 79, 102; development of concept 76–81, 100; financial accounting 78–80; function of 81; legal entity 77–78
Reporting Exchange 88n4
research method: interviewees 4, 5; reporting boundaries 3–5; semi-structured interviews 4

Subject Index

SASB *see* Sustainability Accounting Standards Board (SASB)
scope, term 3, 4
SDGs *see* Sustainable Development Goals (SDGs)
SIC-12 *Special Purpose Entities* 35
significant influence 27, 41n2, 64; definition of 30–31, 47; notion of 48, 50, 56, 65, 80
social management studies, boundaries in 6–11
Solvay **5**, 71–73
special purpose entities, case in financial reporting 34–37
stakeholder democracy 102
Sustainability Accounting Standards Board (SASB) 6, 44, 52; framework 63–64; hybrid approach 75; non-financial reporting 58, 67n3, **94**; materiality 85, 96, 104–105n1; setting reporting boundaries 96–98
sustainability arena 44, 70
sustainability reporting: Global Reporting Initiative (GRI) 45–51; integrated reporting 69–73; non-financial **94**
Sustainable Development Goals (SDGs), United Nations 75–76, 87
symbolic boundaries 7, 101
system boundaries 61–62, 74

Task Force on Climate-related Financial Disclosures (TFCD) 6, 59, 60
Tellus Institute 45
transplantation 18n4; boundaries 2, 15, 16, 97–98; concept of 17, 98, 102; notion of 17–18

transplant theory 16; borrowing and 16–17
Triple Bottom Line Reporting 13
TSC Industries v Northway Inc. (1976) 84

Unicredit 70, 71
United Nations Conference on Trade and Development (UNCTAD) 53, 76
United Nations Environment Programme (UNEP) 45
United Nations Sustainable Development Goals (SDGs) 75–76, 87

value creation 2, 6, 11, 67, 70, 71, 101; definition of **95**; International Integrated Reporting Framework 64–66; process 25, 91, 99; WICI Intangibles Framework 60–64
variable interest entity 35–37, 81
voting interest equity (VIE) model 37

WICI *see* World Intellectual Capital Initiative (WICI)
World Business Council for Sustainable Development (WBCSD) 55
World Economic Forum 51
World Intellectual Capital Initiative (WICI) **5**, 6, 60; Intangibles Reporting Framework 44, 60–64; non-financial reporting **95**
World Resources Institute (WRI) 55

zone of influence 14
zones of conflict 1–2

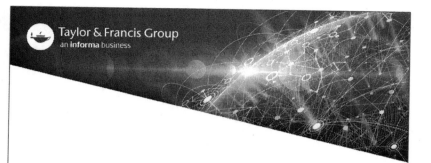